T0362919

PUBLISHED BY BOOM BOOKS

www.boombooks.biz

ABOUT THIS SERIES

.... But after that, I realised that I knew very little about these parents of mine. They had been born about the start of the Twentieth Century, and they died in 1970 and 1980. For their last 20 years, I was old enough to speak with a bit of sense.

I could have talked to them a lot about their lives. I could have found out about the times they lived in. But I did not. I know almost nothing about them really. Their courtship? Working in the pits? The Lock-out in the Depression? Losing their second child? Being dusted as a miner? The shootings at Rothbury? My uncles killed in the War? Love on the dole? There were hundreds, thousands of questions that I would now like to ask them. But, alas, I can't. It's too late.

Thus, prompted by my guilt, I resolved to write these books. They describe happenings that affected people, real people. The whole series is, to coin a modern phrase, designed to push your buttons, to make you remember and wonder at things forgotten. The books might just let nostalgia see the light of day, so that oldies and youngies will talk about the past and re-discover a heritage otherwise forgotten. Hopefully, they will spark discussions between generations, and foster the asking and answering of questions that should not remain unanswered.

BORN IN 1956?

WHAT ELSE HAPPENED?

RON WILLIAMS

AUSTRALIAN SOCIAL HISTORY

BOOK 18 IN A SERIES OF 35 FROM 1939 to 1973

War Babies Years (1939 to 1945):   7 Titles
Baby Boom Years (1946 to 1960):   15 Titles
Post Boom Years (1961 to 1973:   13Titles

BOOM, BOOM BABY , BOOM

BORN IN 1956? WHAT ELSE HAPPENED?

Published by Boom Books.
Wickham, NSW, Australia
Web: www.boombooks.biz
Email: email@boombooks.biz

Creator: Williams, Ron, 1934- author
Title: Born in 1956? : what else happened? / Ron Williams.
ISBN: 9780994601568 (paperback)
Australia--History--Miscellanea--20th century.

Cover images: Mitchell Library

a3236022, Betty Cuthbert; National Archives of Australia:

A12111 8114055 lifesavers;

A1501 8887429 family garden scene. State Library of Victoria

H2004.100/1550, Hoad and Rosewall win Wimbledon.

CONTENTS

BACKGROUND DATA:

Before we barge into 1956, I offer you two pages of data that will help you find your way though the book.

Elizabeth II	Queen of England
Robert Menzies	Prime Minister of Oz
H V (Doc) Evatt	Leader of Opposition
Pope Pius XII	The Pope
Dwight Eisenhower	US President
Anthony Eden	PM of Britain

Winners of the Ashes:

1954-55	England	3 - 1
1956	England	2 - 1
1958-59	Australia	4 - 0

Melbourne Cup Winners:

1955	Toparoa
1956	Evening Peal
1957	Straight Draw

Sydney to Hobart:

1955 winner	Even
1956 winner	Kurrewa IV
1957 winner	Kurrewa IV

Kurrewa IV also won in 1954 and 1960

Davis Cup Winner, 1955 - 57   Australia

PREFACE TO THE SERIES

This book is the 18th in a series of books that I have researched and written. It tells a story about a number of important or newsworthy Australia-centric events that happened in 1956. The series covers each of the years from 1939 to 1973, for a total of thirty five books.

I developed my interest in writing these books a few years ago at a time when my children entered their teens. My own teens started in 1947, and I started trying to remember what had happened to me then. I thought of the big events first, like Saturday afternoon at the pictures, and cricket in the back yard, and the wonderful fun of going to Maitland on the train for school each day. Then I recalled some of the not-so-good things. I was an altar boy, and that meant three or four Masses a week. I might have thought I loved God at that stage, but I really hated his Masses. And the schoolboy bullies, like Greg Favell, and the hapless Freddie Bevan. Yet, to compensate for these, there was always the beautiful, black headed, blue-sailor-suited June Brown, who I was allowed to worship from a distance.

I also thought about my parents. Most of the major events that I lived through came to mind readily. But after that, I realised that I really knew very little about these parents of mine. They had been born about the start of the Twentieth Century, and they died in 1970 and 1980. For their last 20 years, I was old enough to speak with a bit of sense. I could have talked to them a lot about their lives. I could have found out about the times they lived in. But I did not. I know almost nothing about them really. Their courtship? Working in the pits? The Lock-out in the Depression?

Losing their second child? Being dusted as a miner? The shootings at Rothbury? My uncles killed in the War? There were hundreds, thousands of questions that I would now like to ask them. But, alas, I can't. It's too late.

Thus, prompted by my guilt, I resolved to write these books. They describe happenings that affected people, real people. In **1956,** there is some coverage of international affairs, but a lot more on social events within Australia. This book, and the whole series is, to coin a modern phrase, designed to push the reader's buttons, to make you remember and wonder at things forgotten. The books might just let nostalgia see the light of day, so that oldies and youngies will talk about the past and re-discover a heritage otherwise forgotten. Hopefully, they will spark discussions between generations, and foster the asking and the answering of questions that should not remain unanswered.

The sources of my material. I was born in 1934, so that I can remember well a great deal of what went on around me from 1939 onwards. But of course, the bulk of this book's material came from research. That meant that I spent many hours in front of a computer reading electronic versions of newspapers, magazines, Hansard, Ministers' Press releases and the like. My task was to sift out, **day-by-day**, those stories and events that would be of interest to the most readers. Then I supplemented these with materials from books, broadcasts, memoirs, biographies, government reports and statistics. And I talked to old-timers, one-on-one, and in organised groups, and to Baby Boomers about their recollections. People with stories to tell come out of the woodwork, and talk no end about the tragic and funny and commonplace events that have shaped their lives.

The presentation of each book. For each year, the end result is a collection of Chapters on many of the topics that concerned ordinary people in that year. I think I have covered most of the major issues that people then were interested in. On the other hand, in some cases I have dwelt a little on minor frivolous matters, perhaps to the detriment of more sober considerations. Still, in the long run, this makes the book more readable, and hopefully it will convey adequately the spirit of the times.

I have been **deliberately national in outlook**, so that readers elsewhere will feel comfortable that I am talking about matters that affected them personally. After all, housing shortages and strikes and juvenile delinquency involved **all** Australians, and other issues, such as problems overseas, had no State component in them. Overall, I expect I can make you wonder, remember, rage and giggle equally, no matter where you hail from.

POLITICAL BACKGROUND FROM 1955

By the end of 1955, it was obvious to everyone that the Labor Party across the nation was in complete turmoil. For all of that year, it had been battling within itself over where it was going. There were some members who were leaning to the Left, and almost espousing Communism, while there were others whose aims were to remove all traces of Communism from the Party. There were breakaway groups at the States and Federal levels, votes of no confidence in executives and leaders, and it was clear that the whole teeming mass was more involved in self-preservation and petty revenge than in forming and implementing policy.

To top it off, the Party's Leader, Doc Evatt, had recently written to the Soviet's Foreign Minister, Molotov, and asked him in effect whether he had any spies in Australia, and what they were up to. Molotov replied, of course, that he had no such spies. Evatt read the correspondence out in Parliament, and was greeted with howls of derision and laughter from both sides of the House. It was a sad incident, and showed a complete lack of judgement by Evatt. Menzies was happy to accept this unexpected gift, so he called an election forthwith.

He romped it in, and added about 10 seats to his majority. So, he was able to continue his period in office, **not at all worried by his disorganised Opposition**. I will add that Labor stayed in the political wilderness for the next 15 years until GoughWhitlam led them back into the light.

THE INTERNATIONAL FRONT

In major international affairs, Australia followed the American line. This, in the broad scheme of things and for all its faults, was sensible because we needed a big and powerful friend to help us if we were ever attacked. If we stuck to the US when they had their adventures, then we could reasonably expect them to help us if ever we got into strife.

The US was, of course, adamantly opposed to Russia, China, and anything that was painted Red. **Menzies needed no convincing at all on this**, and indeed always gained a lot of political advantage from bringing up the spectre of *Reds Under the Bed* whenever he had half a chance. Time and again, be bashed the Labor Opposition with the insinuation that they were tied to the Communist Party, and this was easy for him, because in fact **Labor was thus tied** through its close links with the Trade Unions. The Red menace might, or it might not, have been a real threat to Australia, but certainly it was a priceless boon politically to the opportunistic Menzies.

Australian troops were gradually being sent to Malaya to combat the insurgency there. The Reds were often seen to be the villains in this, but many of the malcontent Malaysian insurgents there **were simply fighting to be rid of British rule and imperialism**. Our men were slowly being killed and maimed, and this was not a popular intervention back home in Oz. But it was the price that our Government said we had to pay to support the US in their anti-Communist campaign.

There were dozens of nations that were fighting for independence from the pre-war colonial powers such as Britain, France, and the Dutch. One such nation was Egypt, where the locals were getting hot under the collar about the British and their occupation of the zone round the Suez Canal. This matter will come very much to the fore later in this book.

CHANGES IN SOCIETY IN 1955

1955 had been a prosperous year for Australians, and plenty of good things had happened for them. The old six-o'clock swill at the pubs had gone in most States, one-man buses had been introduced over the dead bodies of trade unionists, and dozens of singers from the US visited our shores and sang their songs to adoring, screaming young girls. The Salk vaccine for use against the scourge of polio was introduced, and was being found to be most effective.

There were a few events that were a bit more troubling. There was a lot of talk about how our nation would survive an **atom-bomb attack**. There was also the dawning realisation that **Hire Purchase**, on top of a first and second mortgage, would often bring problems. The famous **Redex round-Australia motor car trial** was now being criticised because of the damage it was doing to humans, roads and wombats. **Clergy were being criticised** for not preaching modern-day sermons, and for not mixing with the general population enough. And **the competition for the design of the Sydney Opera House** was perhaps to be restricted to Australian architects – or was it to be open to all comers?

Then, there were **strikes**. All housewives and all families were at the mercy of a wide range of Trade Unionists who at irregular intervals walked off the job, and stayed away from work for a few days or longer. They wanted more wages, or better working conditions, or safer work places. Sometimes they were justified, and sometimes they were not. But in any case, the general population often found itself without trains, trams, electricity, gas, bread, sanitary services, and other near-essentials that civilised people were accustomed to. Again, we will hear more about strikes as we progress through the year.

Still, even with all these annoyances, times were good, and the number of cars, houses, electric fridges and kids were on the increase. 1955 had been kind to most people, and maybe 1956 would keep up the good work.

BIG EVENTS SCHEDULED FOR 1956

There were two major events that were clearly on the horizon for the year. **The first** was the Olympic Games in Melbourne, starting in November. The Commonwealth was spending a lot of money on the stadia and fields that would be needed for these, and on the infrastructure, and the athletes who would participate. There was already the inevitable media clatter about how the venues were behind schedule, or would be inadequate or dangerous, but for most people this passed with a shrug of the shoulders. At this stage, the preparations were going well, and it looked as if the Games would be both exciting and successful.

The second event was the introduction of TV to the nation, at some time before the Games. A few months ago, there had been a lot of talk about whether we should use the British model (all Government-controlled, like our own ABC) or the American model (with dozens of commercial channels and no ABC). We had opted for a mixed approach, with both the ABC and separate commercial stations. It turned out to be a good mix.

In any case, TV was about to change many of the old habits of this nation. Many old-timers had once said that they would believe in TV when they saw it. **Now** was a good time to start believing.

NOW WE ARE READY TO GO

Well, almost. First, I will tell you the Rules I have used in writing this series. It will help you understand the logic behind my presentation.

MY RULES IN WRITING

NOTE. Throughout this book, I rely a lot on reproducing Letters from the newspapers. Whenever I do this, I put the text in a different font, and indent it a little, and make the font somewhat smaller. I do not edit the text at all. That is, I do not correct spelling or grammar, and if the text gets at all garbled, I do not correct it. It's just as it was seen in the Papers.

SECOND NOTE. The material for this book, when it comes from newspapers, is reported as it was seen at the time. If the benefit of hindsight over the years changes things, then I might record that in my Comments. The info reported thus reflects matters as they were seen in 1956.

THIRD NOTE. Let me also apologise in advance to anyone I might offend. In a work such as this, it is certain some people will think I got some things wrong. I am sure that I did, but please remember, **all of this is only my opinion. And really, my opinion does not matter one little bit in the scheme of things.** I hope you will say **"silly old bugger"**, shrug your shoulders, and read on.

So, now we *are* ready. Let's go. Good luck in 1956.

JANUARY NEWS ITEMS

The **Queen's New Years Honours** included 13 new Australian Knights, among them Richard Boyer, the Chairman of the ABC. A few sportsmen received lesser Honours, including **Harry Hopman** (Davis Cup), and **Keith Miller** and **Ian Johnson** for services to cricket.

January 2nd. Grave new doubts about **whether the new Olympic Stand will be ready for the games in November** were raised today. Both the contractor for the job, and the Unions, believe that the Stand will not be ready, unless of course, **they are given more money to allow overtime**.

NSW Police are studying a system of issuing tickets for motoring offenses (except drink driving). Provision will be made to allow the offender to make payment at the appropriate Centre. Or, if he wishes to defend the case, he must appear in Court on the date set out on the ticket....

This might replace **the current system whereby summonses are issued and all matters are then heard in Court**, a great waste of police time, and the cause of big delays in settlements.

January 10th. **In the 17 days since Christmas, 23 NSW persons have drowned. This is 10 more than the road toll.**

Early warnings of the troubles ahead. The UK and Egypt had an agreement that Britain would withdraw all of her troops from the Suez Canal Zone by June.

The Brits were in fact planning to withdraw by February. This seemed like a good thing....

But now there was talk that they would be replaced by paratroopers stationed at nearby Cyprus, so that they could come to the rescue if trouble occurred in the Zone. **Things are getting muddy in the Egyptian desert.**

January 16th. The Melbourne Cricket Club has agreed to **pay the contractor an extra 20,000 Pounds** to complete the Melbourne Olympic stand "substantially by July." This is not a good precedent to set.

In NSW, and soon after in other States, two big banks (the Bank of NSW and the ANZ) were given permission to **open Savings Banks.** Previously, the only institution that was **allowed to accept deposits** was the Commonwealth Bank. And previously, the activities of those existing banks were confined to big-business borrowing and lending....

The opening of new savings banks would ultimately **allow them to offer housing loans, which had been the sole prerogative of the Commonwealth Bank.** The ending of the Commonwealth's monopoly was great news to many a would-be home-owner.

By January 18th, the number of **NSW drownings since Christmas Eve had increased to 33.**

History was made at a Manly (NSW) surf-carnival when an **all-female team was allowed to join the march-past ceremony.** You doubtless remember the teams of 12-or-so lifesavers marching proudly with their belts, lines and reels. **Question: do they still happen?**

JANUARY GRIPES

One of the good things about January in Australia is that almost everyone goes on holidays and serious work stops. People by the million pick up sticks and go somewhere else. It might be to the shack in the bush, to the caravan or tent by the beach or the lake, or to visit the country or the city relatives. Wherever they go, though, people leave behind most of their worries, and forget that there is an outside world.

So, out come the fishing rods or golf clubs or snorkels. Out go any thoughts about politics and the impending disasters and doom that the newspapers flood us with for the rest of the year. Instead, gallons of tea are drunk, people talk about old times and friends, crosswords are done so long as you can stay awake, and Chinese Checkers give it an Oriental flavour. All of this, of course, before the evening barbie.

However, a few diligent people stay at their writing desks, producing a **never-ending stream of gripes**, and ready to point out to the world that this nation is not yet quite perfect. These worthy people take advantage of the fact that the newspapers too are indolent in January, and will fill their spaces with whatever they can get their hands on. **Gripes** fill this bill perfectly and so, in this month, the Letters columns are filled with lots of complaints and **dubious solutions**.

This year was no exception. I have included a few below. They should give you an early insight into the temper of the times.

NEW YEAR'S HONOURS LISTS

Every year, in January and again in June, the Queen awards Honours to people who have been nominated to her by the Australian Government. The people who receive them are often unknown to most of the public, but they invariably have behind them a considerable record of achievement. Criticism invariably follows these awards, however it is generally not directed at the individuals, but at the system that supports them, and at the concept behind them. The following Letter shows some of this.

Letters, Peter Houlihan. At the start of every year, we wake up to the news that some distinguished Australians have been honoured by the Queen. The people nominated are worthy of praise, and it is good to see them get it.

But there are many others also worthy. They are just as worthy as the recipients and sometimes more so. But somehow the system passes them by. You only have to look at the number of military names, or legal names, in the List to see how certain occupations are always selected.

Are there no plumbers who have done their job above and beyond the call of duty? If a surgeon does many life-saving operations in a life time, he is doing much good. But so too is the dairy farmer who gets up in the morning, in all sorts of weather, every day of the year, and works for hours in stink and mud, with only cows for company. Is he any less valuable for bringing milk to the nation?

I must confess that I can see no easy way to pick out plumbers and dairy farmers for honours. **But I do not have to. Some one else is paid to make the selections.** So, I put it to them, and to you, that we should keep the system, but devise a public debate on what the honours are supposed to achieve, and have the administrators use that policy in making their selections.

Letters, J M Smith. There are some who contend that these honours lists strengthen our ties with Britain; others say they disregard the feelings of our New Australian settlers; while still others say they breed ill-feeling and promote class barriers.

Surely, if genuine commendations are to be made, a new method – essentially Australian in outlook and embracing all politics and peoples – can be devised.

Comment. Mr Smith was ahead of his times in asking **whether** we should have such awards, and suggesting that we need something more appropriate to the local scene. Republicanism in Australia was scarcely heard of in 1956, and loyalty to Britain and the Queen was still mainly an unquestioned act of faith. Most Australians wondered why **they** had missed out again, scratched their heads a little over the selectors' choices, and chuckled over the thought of the sometimes-adventurous Keith Miller receiving such an award from the Queen. Nothing too serious, no harm done.

DOUBTS ON LIQUOR REFORM

NSW had recently changed many of its liquor laws, and other States also had that in hand. One reform was to allow **beer-gardens**, and another allowed groups of 100 or more persons, with a common bond, **to seek a licence to sell grog**. This suited RSL and Workers' clubs, and also sporting clubs.

One major change in NSW was designed to end the 6 o'clock swill. The new laws provided for a break in trading at 6.30pm, and for the re-opening of pubs at 7.30pm.

In general, the new laws were welcomed, despite the slanted comments in the Letter below. The results, too, were that the swill gradually disappeared, that road statistics improved, and public drunkenness was reduced after the police stopped their blitz. But, let this writer have his say.

Letters, R Thompson, NSW Legislative Council. Superintendent Gribble states that 10 o'clock closing has increased road accidents, our short-staffed Police Force is busier than ever, there is considerable judicial comment on drink-caused crime, particularly offences at night, **bodgie-basher attacks** are increasing, the 6 o'clock swill remains, often with a sub-swill at 10 o'clock, and the consumption of alcoholic liquor has risen with extended hotel hours.

In the light of these facts, I am sure that, like myself, many "Herald" readers would like to know **on what your staff correspondent**, who wrote *1955 in Review*, **relies** for the statement, "Liquor reforms (10 p.m. closing) have been tried and found successful."

In the absence of strict enforcement of the liquor laws, and with no alternative proposal, the people, disturbed by the state of the liquor trade and by its resultant social evils and eager for reform, voted in favour of a trial for 10 o'clock closing.

However, no worthwhile reforms of the liquor trade in the community interest will be achieved until proposals are based on the recognition of alcoholic liquor **as a major and growing cause of social evils** – crime, the toll of the road, and, worst of all, broken homes and ruined lives.

Let us drop the tragic farce of treating the liquor problem as a matter of the comfort and convenience of drinkers, acknowledge that it involves us all, and for a start let the people have a say on **reduced alcoholic content of liquor and an effective local referendum on the matter**.

Comment. While the liquor reform laws in NSW passed by a small majority in a referendum, public approval for the changes quickly grew. Later, the so-called meal-break at 6.30pm was abolished, and a few years later, even Sunday trading was approved.

Still, as Mr Thompson's Letter shows, opposition to liquor reform did not suddenly die. Many a Protestant still wanted **a complete ban on the sale of alcohol**, and indeed some of them hold to that line today. Over the years, as further reforms were advocated, these groups persisted in their opposition, and still constitute a strong lobby that has to be considered politically in framing and passing liquor-related laws and regulations.

ICE DELIVERIES

As our world grew more prosperous, many families started to fill their houses with all sorts of appliances, like vacuum cleaners, electric lawn mowers, and electric kettles. By now, the refrigerator had made great inroads into households, replacing old ice-chests. But that is not to say that everyone had a fridge, nor to say that the need for ice as a cooler had disappeared. So this need was met by old-style ice-men with a twice-daily run in summer, who home-delivered to customers, often still with a horse and cart.

But, as you will see below, progress was coming, and with that came some sharp business practices.

Letters, N Johnson, Ice Manufacturers' Association of NSW. You were good enough on Wednesday last to publish some material relative to the fact that some electrical **refrigerator distributors** were **buying ice vending runs** with the aim of withdrawing ice supplies from the public and thus compelling ice-users to purchase domestic refrigerators.

Might I say that this association will take every possible action to maintain ice deliveries wherever they are wanted, and irrespective of any sale by a vendor of his retail territory.

Further, we have served notice that if it should in future be falsely represented to any ice customer that ice deliveries will be withdrawn from any area, this association will immediately take such legal action as our legal advisers might suggest.

Comment. Though, having said that, the days of the ice-men were numbered.

INITIATIONS AT INSTITUTIONS

The Hawkesbury Agricultural College (HAC) was the jewel in the crown of the NSW Department of Agriculture. The college was set in many acres of land, with great facilities for the teaching of agriculture and attracted an annual intake of about 50 students a year. These good-quality students, mainly from the country, would spend three or more years boarding there and emerge thoroughly competent to earn a living on the land.

One requirement of attendance was that the incoming students endure an initiation ceremony that involved doing unusual acts, often to the detriment of their dignity. At the time, many aggregations, of males especially, held such ceremonies, often called bastardisation or initiation, and they were common in the military, in university colleges, and even boarding schools. In the HAC, such ceremonies often lasted for a week, and it was said that they resulted in students accepting the necessary disciplines more quickly, and that they bonded with other students for life as a result. As we will see below, this view was not accepted by everyone.

Controversy emerged from the simple Letter below.

Letters, A Welch. Every year, a new batch of lads are welcomed into the HAC. They arrive there with high hopes, and a firm resolve to make something of themselves, and probably the expectation that they will learn all that is needed to return home to their farms with skills and knowledge they can be proud of.

But from the moment they get there, they are met with the rigours of initiation. They are subjected to humiliation, and taught that this is no place for scholarly learning and the application of science. Instead they are given examples of the degradation that mankind can inflict upon mankind.

This "initiation" goes on for a full week, during which time the new boys are denied any contact with persons outside the college and subjected to a barbarous and disgusting "test" enforced by senior students.

Some of these ordeals are definitely dangerous, and each year some boys are ill or injured as a result. Parents are reluctant to protest for fear their sons will be victimised further.

This brought forth the following response from the **NSW Department of Agriculture**.

Officially, initiation ceremonies at the colleges are not recognised, but there is rigid adherence to the principle that **any activity likely to result in moral, mental or physical harm to students, or to result in damage to clothing or materials, is prohibited.** As a result of long tradition, certain student activities, including initiations, are under the immediate supervision of the Students' Representative Council.

Following an initiation on a recent occasion, all of the first-year students signed a communication which read in part as follows: "This statement is to verify that there was in no way any chance of any one of us having any mental or bodily harm inflicted upon him. In actual fact, the initiation is responsible for a closer and stronger bond of friendship between each of us and as a student body."

The initiation, though unofficial, is also under official control and is well supervised.

It all sounds civilised enough. Just a few boys horsing around, having fun. But it was more than that. Dozens of Letters flooded into the Sydney Morning Herald (*SMH)*, and it was clear that the subject was one that stirred many passions and worries.

Firstly, let me give you an extract that described in part some of the activities forced on the new students.

Letters, INTERESTED OBSERVER. In Dr Noble's efforts to keep things quiet, there was no mention of the use of entrails from the slaughter-house, or the enforced chewing of animal testicles, which is both disgusting and unhygienic as the vile objects are passed from student to student.

No mention was made of the eating of soap, or the compulsion to perform continuous physical jerks, or of such pleasant tests as crawling over heaps of blue metal.

There were other Letters that weighed in with different thoughts, but were clearly opposed to the system.

Letter, Ex-Student's Parent, NSW country. "No damage to clothes, no damage mentally, physically, or in any other way!"

Never shall I forget the shock I received when I saw my son at the end of this dreadful week. He was a lad used to hard farm work, and therefore far better fitted physically to stand the "grueling" than many. He had lost almost half a stone in weight and was utterly exhausted, both mentally and physically. The case of clothes he brought home was beyond describing, the filth and smell were disgusting.

Of course all students sign a statement verifying all the things mentioned by Dr Noble, but have they any choice if they wish to avoid further trouble? I think this is not very likely.

Letter, J S. It is interesting to note the assumption that cruelty and humiliation whether in a minor form, as in this case, or in their worst form as seen in Nazi or Japanese concentration camps, have a beneficial effect on the character of those who suffer them.

I do not think this view would be held by many psychologists today, nor would they believe that any good whatever is done to the character of the people who inflict the cruelty.

Admittedly qualities of endurance and amazing courage were shown by most of the victims, but these qualities were surely there already.

Letter, Parent, NSW country. May I make a plea for the smaller lads about to face up to their secondary education in boarding-schools?

At 11 years of age, my own son faced this ordeal and till this day – six years later, I have not heard the whole of the sordid details of his group's initiation, but I do know that these lads had intimate parts of their bodies blackened with boot polish and their heads flushed in a cistern. Fear of victimisation held them silent, though now it may possibly be regarded as a joke, it most certainly created a complex that will be hard to forget. In reply to Colin Smith's letter upholding initiation ceremonies as a solution to the bodgie problem, I would like to point out that sadism and violence are the hallmarks of bodgie-ism, as any police officer will verify.

Any body of students who "gang up" to inflict sadistic and violent acts upon their fellow (and junior) students immediately place themselves in the same class as bodgies and delinquents.

Letter, John R W Wood. Since its inception, the initiation has become more imaginative, more out of order to the detriment of its true significance. Now, according to latest reports, it has become close to animal savagery.

Certain aspects of the initiation can be classified as an exhibition of fetish, savagery, revenge and unbridled primitive behaviour that is quite out of place in a modern educational institution.

But, as usual, there were quite a few who supported it.

Letter, Colin R Smith. As a recent ex-student, I would be extremely surprised if Mr Kennard could find three objectors among the entire number of students and hundreds of ex-students.

This initiation treats all students alike, and brings about an equality among lads whose parents range from prosperous graziers and doctors to Laborers and pensioners and widows and widowers.

Contrary to Mr Kennard's contention, most of the college staff favours the initiation, because they can see its purpose achieved. They cannot express their opinions publicly however, because interfering people who only know half of the story have influenced the policy of the Department of Agriculture.

If every Sydney youth were so fortunate as to attend Hawkesbury College and undergo its worthy, traditional initiation, the bodgie problem of which we hear so much lately would be unknown.

Letter, M J Gallagher. The initiation is not entirely thought up by the third year students. Before it is carried out, a complete report of what the initiation is to consist of has to be (or was in my time) handed to the college authorities for approval. Anything considered dangerous or more humiliating than should be is omitted. Naturally, the third year students are held responsible for anything that should go amiss.

The main thing in favour of the ceremony is that it brings about a great spirit of goodwill between new students and those in the two senior years. I made more friends in that first week than I would have made during the whole of the first year otherwise.

A number of graduates from the program wrote to say that they had gone through the initiation, and that it had helped them settle in. They were of the opinion that young men needed some family substitute in their first days away from home, and that the robustness of the physical activity stopped them from moping round.

Along the same lines, one parent, Mr Mobbs, was confident that the tests were well-planned, and carefully executed, and that the administration was on the ball supervising from afar at all times. He admits the tests were tough, but expects boys of that age and inclination to not be worried by that. In fact, from his experience with many boys, the lads enjoyed the physical challenge that allowed them to prove themselves to themselves in the wider world.

Comment. I appreciate that initiation ceremonies are good for breaking the ice among incoming groups of strangers. Some people describe the process as cutting the umbilical cord, or breaking away from the apron strings. In any case, they can be pleasant experiences and beneficial in getting down to business quickly.

But it is easy to see how they can get out of hand, and approach barbarity. They can become events where bullies force supposed weaklings to kowtow to their superior position, and **then** they are hard to support.

Still, they persist. Sixty years later, the newspapers carry stories of such ceremonies in the military, and the hushed-up abuses therein. I suspect it is all part of the age-old Establishment story, where the holders of power want to demonstrate to possible challengers that it is **they** who are the bosses. But, at the same time, it reflects the resilience of high-spirited youth that energetically craves excitement and thrills.

NEWS FROM THE BATTLEFIELD

Penang, Malaya. Australian troops waiting in ambush shot dead their Queensland sergeant. They mistook him for a terrorist. He was the **first Australian soldier to die** in battle in the war against Malayan terrorists.

FEBRUARY NEWS ITEMS

Something to look forward to. Britain's Atomic Weapons Establishment announced that **a three-decker H-bomb will be tested somewhere in the Pacific next year.** This is the most powerful type of bomb in the world. This was to maintain parity with the US and the Reds in the USSR....

If other countries object to a ground test, the bomb will be exploded about four miles up in the air so that the fireball will not touch the earth's surface....

It seems there will be few safety concerns – **in Britain.**

Adelaide. A fight between twin brothers led to the murder of one, and the suicide of the other at a camp 80 miles east of Adelaide. Police believe the brothers brawled to the death in their timber-cutting hut in desolate mallee scrub....

One brother **killed the other with an axe after battering him insensible, then walked six miles to the river and drowned himself.** At one spot near their hut, the earth for about 6 feet was churned four inches deep where the brothers had fought with fist, boots, and mallee logs.

The Australian trotting industry at this time held a **big carnival each year called the Inter-Dominion Pacing Championship** that saw our own trotters and those from New Zealand clash in a programme of eight races. It drew big crowds (31,000 this year) to Sydney's Harold Park, and gambling on it was Australia-wide....

The trotting boom continued for 30 years. Since then it has gone into decline. Harold Park has given way to medium density housing, and attendances at provincial tracks has fallen to a handful of say 1,000 die-hards....

This is an example of an industry that was well run, except for the occasional rogue steward or driver, that **went into decline simply because of social changes.**

Czech wrestler Emil Koroschenko was thrown out of the ring at **a wrestling match in a bout at Sydney's White City last night.** He was taken to hospital, and found to have five fractured ribs.   His opponent was **32-stone** King Kong. At their previous bout, Koroschenko had smashed a chair over King Kong's head, crippling him for several months.....

This old-style wrestling is **another industry that was blown away by the winds of social change.**

Albert Pierpont has been **Britain's public hangman** for over a decade. He has hanged many famous people, for example, Lord Haw Haw in 1946. As a full time job, he owns and operates the Rose and Crown Hotel in Poole in England....

On February 18th, the British House of Commons voted to abolish hanging for murder. Albert accepted the news philosophically, and said he was doing quite well from the pub. He pointed out that he received 15 Pounds for each hanging he did. He also said that hanging was in the family, and that **his father and uncle were hangmen.** Here is another industry which was crippled by lack of demand and by **changing regulations.**

GROWING TRADE CONCERNS

England and Australia were starting to adjust to the realities of trading in the post-war era. Until now, the entire Empire had stuck together in a giant cartel that kept every one of them safe from outside competition in certain products.

Let me over-simplify, by talking about wheat. We had lots of wheat, and the Brits needed a lot more than they could produce. So they bought wheat from us. But there were other countries out there which were ready to sell wheat, and some of them could land it in Britain at a smaller cost then we could.

Yet the Poms said that they would take much of their wheat from Australia. Why would they do that? Because we said that **in return** we would take some of their products, again at a somewhat higher cost to us, as the quid pro quo. As part of this comfy arrangement, the contracts for the deals were for long periods such as five years, and this meant that people like the wheat growers could plan their lives and production well in advance.

This was called the "preference" system, and it applied to much of our agricultural produce. The other countries of the British Empire lived by the same rules, both in relation to Britain, but also to every other nation in the Empire.

By 1956, though, things were changing. For example, Argentina was quite happy to sell beef and fruit at lower than the Australian prices, and was doing so in European countries. So the cry in Britain went out demanding that these cheaper goods be let into Britain. What was stopping that? The **preference system**.

So the next cry was, let's get rid of the preference system. That sounded good for the British buyer, but what about their exporters? Australia was sure to retaliate if the Brits took less of our goods. And anyway, the Brits were locked long-term into Australia.

So, the whole matter was just now coming into focus. Should Britain dump the preference system? At the same time, there were voices, small as yet, saying that the Brits should do just that, and that Europe should set up their own preference system, **a common market**. Should Britain's future be tied up with such an institution? Surely, if it turned out that way, it would mean that the Empire countries would be cast adrift, and the Empire would collapse. **What about that, mate?**

Arguments along these lines were emerging in 1956. They had a long way to go, but it was becoming clear in Australia that the good old days of within-Empire trading were under threat, and that we might even have to start selling our goods elsewhere. This was a much tougher proposition.

The population of Australia was not too concerned about all this. To most people, it seemed a long way off, it was stuff that **might** happen, and probably would have no effect at all for a long time. But there were a few people, including our Trade Minister, Black Jack McEwen, who realised that it meant tougher times ahead, and for our agricultural industries in particular. The writings of some concerned citizens made the Papers.

Maxwell Newton of Harbord was an up-and-coming writer and financial guru who went on to fame for his erudite writings. He attacked McEwen for the wooliness of his thinking and negotiating, and for the lack of clarity in his arguments with the UK.

In the current dispute over the dumping of Argentine apples and pears in England, he criticised arguments based on the sentimental attachments we mutually have with Britain, and the claim that if we do not **sell** in Britain, then we won't have the money to **buy** from Britain.

He points out that the British Board of Trade has negotiators who are experienced, tough, and right on the ball. He argues that McEwen is too nice to them, and is not pressing some carefully thought out plan on them. Such a plan, Newton says, must bring benefits to both parties. If that approach is used, the wise heads opposite will agree, and then changes can be made.

He thinks McEwen also needs to take off the gloves and point out to the Brits that they are in a desperate position, and need Australian goods more than we need their trade. Going and crying for mercy will not move the hard heads at all.

The fact is that neither McEwen nor the Prime Minister is prepared to put pressure on the Brits.

Comment. In effect, he says we are too wishy-washy in our trade talks, and need to toughen up.

Letter, Observer. We live in a vast country and our small population is saturated with powerful trade-unionism. We have over-full employment, and wages have been forced up far beyond the value of their produce by world standards. Our currency is consequently depreciated and has lost purchasing power.

We are disappointed now because world markets are not prepared to accept many of our goods at our prices.

More than that, we object to anybody else disposing of their products at rates cheaper than our own.

It is surely time we learned that **the Golden Age is over** and that our comparatively small working force can never expect to be able to call the price tune for the world of trade outside our borders. Only in time of war – if we are lucky – can we hope to get away with that.

We must work as the rest of the world has to work or shut up shop.

Today, as before, cheap food and fuel for power are the keys to economic stability, opening the door to trade in easy competition with other nations. It is unfortunate that in this land of plenty we **have neither of these two essentials**, for we ourselves pay through the nose for everything, even our own local produce, with pounds that lose purchasing value every day.

Comment. Here was a second cry to toughen up, but I suspect it was not **yet** heard by many.

THE PERPETUAL HOUSING SHORTAGE

When WWII started, the nation's resources were taken away from normal living and instead used for defence purposes. This meant that building materials for houses were virtually not available. As well as this, the Federal and State Governments were worried about inflation, and thought they could avoid it by freezing the rents on houses. So they did just that, and from about 1941, **landlords could not raise the rents** they charged without impossible-to-get government approval.

Other restraints on **existing** landlords applied, but they applied equally well to **prospective** landlords. This meant that the people who had been investing in **building** housing in the past were no longer willing to do that. So this, combined with the shortage of building materials, meant that from 1941, virtually no rental housing was built.

Believe it or not, the same regulations on landlords still applied in full, in most States, in 1956. The reason was purely political. There was a very large body of electors who were renting their houses, and doing so happily with a rent that was fixed at 1940 levels. There was also a number of landlords who were unhappily collecting 1940-level rents. But **the number of renters far outweighed the number of landlords**, so what government would be prepared to lose so many votes by letting rents rise? The answer was that no government so far had done so, even after ten years of peace-time normal conditions. In fact, it was only in 1965 and thereafter that governments really start to bite this bullet, so that the glory days for renters continued for another decade after 1956.

Peter Clyne, from Sydney, was a flamboyant Sydney solicitor. He was not terribly conformist, nor was he shy of being heard in public. He gained his own form of notoriety by tax avoidance. He wrote 21 books, mainly on that topic, and among other sometimes-challenging activities, was declared a bankrupt twice.

He noted that the NSW Government had recently said it intended **to extend** the system of rent control, and questioned its intentions towards its sister Landlord and Tenant Act.

He pointed out that the landlord had seen no income increase since about 1939, but tenants' incomes **had increased three-fold**. He went on to point out that a **new owner** of a tenanted dwelling could not take possession of it until 18 months had elapsed. Even then, it is **he** who must find alternative **satisfactory** accommodation for the tenant.

He went on to say that with **housing** disputes in courts, **both** parties must pay their own legal costs. **In other courts**, the loser mainly pays the costs of the other parties, but not so here. This allows a wealthy party to stall and stall in the courts, knowing full well that the other party will lose their nerve as the costs mounted.

Letters, Mary Toner, Brisbane and Adelaide. Mr Clyne's comments about housing rang a bell with me. I have recently moved from Adelaide to Brisbane and have looked at both housing markets. Without going into detail, let me point out that Mr Clyne's problems are mirrored in the other two States.

How politicians can sleep at night, I do not know. Apart from the obvious injustices to landlords, they are **inhibiting the building of new dwellings,** so that if we **can** get a house in Brisbane, it will be run-down and some of them should be condemned.

Surely some of them must have the brains to know that the few votes they will get now from tenants must certainly be more than balanced by the votes from ordinary people who want good housing and lots of it.

Letters, Elizabeth Randall. The law even gives tenants the right **to make money from sub-letting**. This is bad, as all privilege should carry with it a corresponding responsibility, and there is thus engendered in tenants a complete disregard for the care of the property they live in.

The good landlord, anxious to append money on improving and maintaining his property, will not do it because he is saddled with bad tenants, often not of his own will, and very often sub-tenants and invitees of his tenants. He knows his money is wasted. And so we see a decent property fall into ruin and the landlord is powerless.

On the other hand, a decent tenant, often lodged in residentials with rapacious harpies for landlords, is subject to many petty and ingenious forms of persecution if he goes to the law for protections against exploitation.

What good does a judicial order do him if he finds his washing trampled into the ground when he returns from work, his light and gas unaccountably failing, and other things to make life a misery?

I suggest most good landlords would welcome, even more than rental increases, **the right to obtain possession** where a tenant has broken any clause of his tenancy agreement. It should be **mandatory** for a magistrate to make an order where such a case is proven, but at present the magistrate has discretion.

Comment. The conducts mentioned in this last Letter were not rare. Such actions, and the arguments they provoked, were the subject of much discussion at barbies and dinner parties.

NATURAL CHILDBIRTH

Back in 1936 in Britain a medical doctor, Grantly Dick Read, was hitting the headlines from a book advocating **natural childbirth**. Now, his methods had been re-discovered in New York, and were flowing through to Australia. A Special Article by a *SMH* reporter looked at the technique.

He wrote that ideally it involved as little interference with the birthing process as possible, including no anaesthetic and no surgery. It required that the woman **be educated in advance to remove her fear of childbirth**, and that she be cognisant of physical exercises that she should do between contractions to relax her muscles.

In one of Read's books, he wrote that "girls, from the time they are knee-high, are frightened by their mothers (and maiden aunts) with the notion that it is terribly painful to have a baby. This exaggerated fear tenses the muscles of the uterus. Result: Pain. The pain multiplies the fear, and a vicious fear-tension cycle begins." His solution was to remove the fear through education, and to teach exercises that reduce the tension.

This interesting article brought forth many responses.

Letters, Maureen Degenhardt. As one who has experienced a natural birth with a first baby, I consider this is the right of every woman. Therefore I must challenge such statements by a prominent obstetrician such as: "The average woman was neither capable of, nor wanted, natural childbirth", and "it is **suitable only for the intelligent person**." I consider that the average woman is intelligent and is quite capable of having a natural birth providing the confinement has no complications. The only reason why the average woman today is not practising natural childbirth is because she is not encouraged to or does not know of the method.

If both doctors and hospitals acquainted their patients with the procedure of natural childbirth, recommended reading material and encouraged them to do the relaxation exercises, it would take up very little of their valuable time and yet set many women on the way to the happy birth of their babies.

Some hospitals in Sydney do have prenatal exercise classes and lectures but even where this is so, the patient does not receive the instruction and encouragement necessary during the actual Labor.

I agree that it is impracticable for a doctor to stay with a patient for 12 hours. However, it is possible for him to be with the patient longer than just the delivery period, as is the accepted thing. On the other hand, if the nurses were trained in Dr Grantly Dick Read's method as part of their obstetrics course, they would then be able to instruct and assist the patient during the stages of Labor.

Let's give the average woman the opportunity of having a natural birth and see if she is capable of it – don't discourage her from even trying by telling her she is not intelligent enough.

Letters, Mother of Three. I read thoroughly and practised thoroughly the art outlined by Dr Grantly Read, and was assisted throughout by a nurse specially assigned to my case before and during birth. The method was a complete and utter failure for me, and this was not because I was unable or unwilling to learn, or physically or mentally incapable of carrying out the methods recommended.

As a normal average university graduate, I think I would have had the necessary background to make a reasonably intelligent approach to the subject, and to afford the required cooperation.

By all means let expectant mothers try the methods recommended – no harm can result – but have **their normal anaesthetics** nearby in case the charm does not work.

Letters, Margaret McCarthy. Dr Read never maintained that the doctor need "hold the patient's hand for 12 hours." He merely asserted that she should not be left alone for long periods, for solitude was likely to build up fears, the main enemy of relaxation.

The difficulties of implementing Dr Read's theories, in a vast institution like Paddington's Women's Hospital, are obvious, but is it necessary for them to go so far in the opposite direction? I went in hoping to be able to relax on my own, but it would have needed a will of iron.

In my own country hospital I was curtly told I was not allowed to read, and I must turn off the bed-light. The sister in charge discouraged all conversation. There was enough light to see the clock, unfortunately.

Letters, Elie Wilson. The one thing that would have helped me relax would have been the presence of my husband. But, in three births at three different hospitals, my husband has been excluded on "matron's orders."

If you want natural births, simply allow fathers to attend when the couple ask for him. Then the birthing will be kept in perspective, and the bogy of pain will be seen for what it is – that is, some predictable pain for a short period.

NEWS AND VIEWS ON DOGS

Letters, R Bowell. Last year one of your correspondents asserted that his suburb had more mongrel dogs than any other suburb in Sydney. I would like to issue a challenge, both as to number and variety of mongrels, on behalf of North Balgowlah.

We have the obvious crosses between Great Danes and every known breed of Spaniel and we also have rarer crosses between Border Collies and French Poodles. Between them they yelp most of the day, and make the nights hideous in an otherwise peaceful suburb.

Letters, Woof Woof. I deplore the snobbery of your correspondent, R Bowell, in implying that only mongrel dogs are a barking nuisance.

In Strathfield, for instance, pedigree dogs, which number thousands, have a right royal time. Some "good living" owners are sporting enough to go out and leave them for hours to shatter people's nerves.

A dog down the street lives outside his gate, rushing cars and motor bikes and pedestrians, and splitting the whole night with noise.

I, and the dogs of Strathfield, would be happy to accept any competition, day or night.

Letters, Edward Currie, Davenport. I have a poultry farm on the outskirts of town. Unfortunately, some of my sheds are close to the road, so that thefts have been common in the past. I fixed this by getting six large unhappy dogs. I put them in six kennels around the sheds late at night. If anything moves during the night, they bark their heads off.

This is music to my ears. I have no thefts for two years since I bought the dogs.

Letters, John Stockman. Having worked blue cattle dogs for years and heard many complaints that pedigreed stock are not usually good workers (and cattle dogs are primarily a working dog), I went last year to the Show at Adelaide to see the "blues" being judged.

No wonder they have a bad reputation as workers. The majority looked like cross-bred Alsatians, either black or dirty white in colour. Others had the appearance of a bulldog. Where has the low-set, solid but agile, hard-biting blue gone?

To be of any use to cattlemen the dog must be low set, agile and solid. I saw a few very nice dogs there, but most of those filled only minor placings, and were regarded by most breeders as "too small for show dogs." The working cattle dog is a part of Australia but bears little resemblance to the dogs winning major awards at some of our shows.

The colour does not affect a dog's working ability but the breed's colour is blue and, as the wrong colour is counted against dogs of other breeds (including other working breeds), why shouldn't the wrong colour count against the cattle dog?

Is it not time, before the breed disappears, that points for and against this beautiful, alert, and wholly Australian dog were reviewed and a new show standard set, taking into consideration that it is a working dog, a blue dog?

NEWS AND VIEWS

Victoria rejected 10 o'clock pub closing at a vote, by a large majority. This means that 6 o'clock closing, recently abandoned in NSW, will remain in place in Victoria. **That suggests it will still be in place for the Olympic Games.**

A strong rumour swept Canberra that **Mr Menzies was about to resign** as Prime Minister. It turned out to **be wrong – by almost 10 years**.

MARCH NEWS ITEMS

1,000 yelling fans met American entertainer Nat King Cole at Sydney's Mascot Airport. There was the usual pushing and shoving, a big glass door and a window were broken, and a dozen Special Police were busy for a hectic two hours keeping control. **This was all very normal for the arrival of top US stars.**

In the various States, agitation **for three weeks annual leave** for workers under State awards is growing stronger and it seems that the Labor Party in Queensland will **add it to its platform for the upcoming State elections.**

March 12th. The famous **conductor of the Sydney Symphony Orchestra, Sir Eugene Goossens**, was interrogated by police when he arrived back in Australia from London. Police and Customs Officers searched his bags at Sydney Airport, **and seized 1,000 photographs, and four rubber masks and three books.** The Sunday *Sun-Herald* added that the books supposedly "dealt with sex matters." The police and Goossens remain tight-lipped on the reason for the search.

Russian Olympic Games officials arrived in Darwin and said that **Russia would send 450 athletes to the Games.** They expected that they would compete in every event, and **hoped to win more medals than previously….**

This confirmed **a rapidly developing trend** to make **the Games a test of national prowess**, rather than focus on athletes as individuals. **The USA also was taking the national-pride approach.**

The price of beer across the nation will rise by about two pence for a 10-ounce glass. **The Feds announced an increase in sales tax, effective immediately, and it applies to tobacco, cars, and spirits.** The aim was to reduce the budget deficit.

March 23rd. **Sir Eugene Goossens was convicted** and fined the maximum penalty of 100 Pounds in the Court of Petty Sessions. **He had imported prohibited goods, namely obscene photographs and literature.** His barrister, agreed that a very grave offence had taken place

Mr Shand went on to say, mysteriously, that **the material was brought into the country "as a result of threats."** He said the matter was under investigation, and he hoped the nature of these investigations would become apparent soon. In fact, no clarification was ever offered....

Prior to the Court hearing, Goossens was **temporarily relieved of his duties as conductor of the Orchestra** at his own request, through ill health.

The Anglican Archbishop of Sydney, Dr Mowll, said yesterday that it wa**s depressing to find that the first prize in a Tasmanian lottery** had been won by a Sydney syndicate. He went on to say that the tickets cost 100 Pounds each and the first prize was 100,000 Pounds....

"The growth of this type of gambling can have nothing but an injurious effect on the nation." Dr Mowll **He called on the people to turn their minds from gambling and other social and moral evils, to God.**

JOHNNIE RAY IS BACK

Johnnie came to Oz last year, and CRIED to big Sydney audiences. He escaped with his life from thousands of screaming teenage girls, and then decided he would like a return bout. So he landed in Sydney again on 5th of March.

This, as it turned out, was a mistake, because it was a Sunday. That meant that 40,000 school-girls had no problems in getting to Sydney airport. Once there, they did their normal thing of screaming, pushing, swooning and the like. No real problem that the 22 police officers there could not handle.

Then Johnnie came out of Security. He said he wanted to meet his fans. And so he did. The waiting crowd stampeded. It carried away the barriers set up outside the overseas terminal lounge, and bore him to the ground. He was crushed against a wall, and carried from the terminal entrance into the middle of the crowd. Six policemen came to his rescue, and lifted him shoulder-high and forced their way through massed teenagers, back to the safety of the terminal.

Ray was gasping for breath, a new shantung suit was torn in places, and his wrist watch was torn off. He lay dormant for two minutes, and kept asking "What happened? What happened?" Airport officials, who were quite accustomed to these so-called welcomes to US stars of screen and stage, described the welcome as the most hysterical and disgusting that they had ever seen.

Still, Ray was on his feet in a few more minutes, and was taken out a back entrance and went his weary way. The publicity he got from the incident was worth a fortune, and he was talented enough to capitalise on this. He had a great tour Down Under.

OUR TOURISM INDUSTRY

The above heading is a bit misleading. Really, we had no such industry. A few brave big hotels in the big cities, the sporadic promotion of the Melbourne Cup with overseas models, and the occasional bally-hoo with sporting teams visiting the nation, was about the best we could muster.

Those overseas tourists who braved our hotels and dunnies and cafes and litter-strewn highways and parks and roads and trains were unanimous in saying that the nation's people were great, and our facilities were terrible. **Let me pick out our hotels, for example.** Our publicans were, with only a few exceptions, sellers of beer only. Our brewers, the owners of the pubs, were also sellers of beer. Accommodation and decent toilets and meals and airy clean premises were not on their agenda. Neither was politeness nor any sign that the customer is always right. A night in a country pub, or a suburban pub, was an occasion to be remembered and laughed about over the week-end dinner table.

One writer noted that recently some Americans had announced an interest in building big hotels in Australia, and that two big shipping companies had promised to build two liners for Australia-US travel. He spoke out about the obvious need to gain overseas dollars by promoting tourism.

Letters, Reeve Farrow. The only constructive proposal from the Australian Government has been for an export drive to **sell our tariff-protected manufactures** which they must have known would be impossible to sell at a profit and, indeed, hard to give away to overseas countries for the mere cost of their transportation.

The economies of several European countries, including France, **are virtually based on the tourist industry,** while the governments of the UK, South Africa, Canada, and New Zealand have long recognised its considerable importance as a source of external income.

But, apparently, the minds of our leaders have never quite got round to the highly important fact that, in the tourist industry, we have an "export" which – if handled with the courage, capital, and capacity it deserves – could solve our external economic problem and lead to development in Australia, over the next decade, to an extent never previously envisaged.

Comment. The task of developing tourism was, however, enormous. Everywhere you looked, something was wrong, or dirty or neglected, or just not there at all. Let me illustrate with the Letter below about Jenolan Caves House. This guest house was (and is) a true tourist attraction. It is set in thousands of acres of wild terrain, the only dwelling for tens of miles, and boasts access to a magnificent complex of caves. The writer tells us though that the House itself was not at all magnificent.

Letters, Tourist. While we deplore the lack in certain hotels of wash basins for customers, it is alarming to see the position in the State Government-owned Jenolan Caves House.

Here a person is expected to spend a holiday **for a week or so**, and there is not even the basic essential of a wash basin installed in the room. If the guest wishes to clean his teeth or do his hair, he must go to the common bathroom and use the basin that all the guests must use. It is amazing to find, when shown your room, that the wall and ceiling are badly disfigured by water stains from the rain seeping through.

Furthermore, in such a remote area, not the slightest effort is made as regards the entertainment of the guest within the house. With more interest in the entertainment and comfort of the guest, this spot would be a magnificent place for a holiday.

To illustrate further, I enclose two Letters on the fundamental issue of hygiene.

Letters, L W Gill. On a recent trip in the Riverina Express, an air-conditioned train with many excellent features designed to attract travellers and tourists, I wanted to wash my hands in the men's toilet. There was a basin but no soap to be seen. A metal container might have contained liquid soap, but I did not know how to get at it. It could not be tipped and there was no push button to expel the soap.

Finally, the conductor told me that the underside of the container was shaped like a nozzle. If you want soap, rub your hand across the nozzle. Some soap from inside adheres to the skin. Keep on rubbing till you get enough for a wash. The state of any hands that used the contrivance, before you, is immaterial.

On many of these stations [Springwood, Lawson, Wentworth Falls, Katoomba] the toilet facilities were being remodeled. I wrote to the acting chief manager saying that not one station had a wash basin in the men's toilet. As the stations were at tourist centres, I asked whether he would support a recommendation to provide at least one wash basin in each men's toilet. I was told no support could be expected for such an extravagance.

Letters, Alex Court. Is it too much to ask that on the dining cars of all daylight expresses, there should be a hygienic and sterilising contrivance for washing up crockery and cutlery? Under present conditions, any pleasure one might derive from a meal is destroyed by the unpleasant sight of waitresses, on the other side of the counter, washing up the dirty dishes of earlier diners in lukewarm water, and wiping them with a tea towel that is not discarded until it is so soggy as to be useless.

It is disappointing to describe any Government department in such terms, particularly to one who, like myself, was an officer in the department for nearly 40 years.

Comment. On top of the shortage of facilities and cleanliness, this nation **then** had something of an attitude problem. I think it is well accepted **now** that, in the tourist trade, employees have to keep a civil tongue in their heads, and accept the vagaries of tourists with good grace. Back in 1956, our concept that all-men-are-equal made us collectively not quite so subservient, and any tourist with an air of superiority was asking for a quick put-down. Which means that our local lads and lasses were sometimes seen to be quite rude. That was not good for tourism.

CRUELTY TO SHARKS

Letters, Disgusted. While at Watson's Bay last Saturday, my husband and I watched while a 12ft shark caught by some big-game fishermen was weighed upon the official metal weighing platform of the Big Game Fishermen's Association. After its weight and measurements had been recorded (12ft, 715lb), the shark was left hanging by its tail to die.

While none of us hold any brief for sharks, I think those caught should be mercifully put out of their agony.

It is revolting and bad for children and others to watch the agony of such a monster, and the vomit and blood which is brought up because it is hanging in such a position. To me this is unsportsmanlike and sadistic.

Game fishing was a sport that was appreciated by the rich, because of the high cost of pursuing it. Zane Grey, the famous American writer of wild-west novels was a regular participant, often visiting Queensland. Well-known radio personality, Bob Dyer, similarly dabbled.

Most Western nations were affiliated with a world body that set stringent rules for the fishermen, and definite standards of conduct for the disposal of their catches. Weigh-in stations were at the right spots in all capital cities, and at strategic points along the coast. Catches were closely monitored and weighed so as to reduce wild stories. All of this was true of Australia.

So, when the above Letter was published, the big fishermen in the nation were quick to defend their sport. It became obvious there were many different matters to consider.

Letters, Game Fisherman.   "Disgusted" thinks it cruel to see sharks caught by game fishermen alive on the weighing station at Watson's Bay.

All sharks are smacked over the snout with a heavy implement when caught, but this is by no means an easy task in a rough sea with a big shark.

As a rule this does finish them off, but some are more-or-less alive when brought in. In the case of a mako shark, it is very hard to stop it from wriggling or snapping when brought in.

Although sharks often do this, in some cases it is purely muscular action, and the fish is probably dead.

However, as a game fisherman, I have long deplored the rule which disqualifies a fisherman should he harpoon, lance, or shoot a shark before it is weighed.

The rule is made to stop a fisherman shooting a shark, and then hauling it in to claim he caught it fairly. It is high time, however, that this rule was amended to allow the shark to be lanced after it has been caught, in accordance with the rules, and witnessed by the fisherman's boatman.

Quite apart from whether it is cruel or not, the present practice is certainly dangerous, not so much to the fishermen, who are used to handling these sharks, but to the general public who crowd around and try to prise open the jaws.

In spite of repeated warnings, children and adults will not keep away.

Letters, Kerwin Maegraith. On many occasions I was the companion of the late Zane Grey on his ocean salt-water big game angling trips, and during that time the renowned American hauled in some mighty monsters of the deep.

Never did the famous angler allow his catch to be hung on the weighing hoist until he was completely satisfied it was dead, and a large mallet was kept for the purpose of killing the fish.

I don't doubt some of the contemporary deep-sea fishermen are now breaking the rules in this regard.

The rules of game fishing are as well laid down as those of cricket and of Rugby football. One of them is that your catch must be killed and not left in agony on the hoist.

Letters, A Watkins. One might ask: When is an animal dead? It is known that human hair will grow after death. A pulsating piece of chicken heart can be grown outside the body even for months. In the case of cold-blooded animals, the tissues retain their vitality a long time.

Another point worth considering is whether movements in an animal indicate suffering. You can remove the brain from a frog, yet if you put a drop of acid on its skin, it will try to wipe off the irritant and will writhe apparently purposefully in a manner very painful to watch. Yet it feels nothing, the movements being due only to spinal reflexes.

Your correspondent who thinks sharks can be killed by a blow on the snout is indulging in very wishful thinking. Ask a well-known Sydney game fisherman whose boat was nearly wrecked when a mako shark, which was so treated, developed tantrum aboard subsequently! The blows quieten the shark but only some die afterwards without recovering.

I have been big-game fishing for 25 years under strictest rules, but know nothing of those rules another correspondent cites as stating that game fish must be killed. On the contrary the big-game rules strictly forbid mutilation.

In spite of my belief that sharks may be unconscious or suffering little when on the hoist, I am entirely in sympathy with the Newcastle angler who would like the rule against mutilation relaxed.

But how far each angler would consider his duties went is problematical. If carried out sufficiently thoroughly to satisfy all, the resultant mess and smell on the weighing-station would probably set afire a fresh train of correspondence.

Comment. I suggest to you that, the next time you catch a 15-foot shark, you think carefully before you finish it off. No matter what you do, you could offend someone.

WHAT'S HAPPENING TO THE ECONOMY

Bob Menzies and his Treasurer, Arthur Fadden, were worried by the direction of the nation's economy. They knew that in future there could well be disruption if the Brits decided that Empire preference was finished, but in the immediate term inflation was hitting the headlines. As usual, when an economic predicament arises, they had the choice of putting the breaks on by raising taxes and tariffs. Or, they could spend more as a government and hope to stimulate the economy so that people produced more and took the pressure off inflation.

They, as they always did both before and after this time, went for the austerity mode. Not too severely. Instead they just raised some sales taxes and put increased excise on beer, tobacco, cars and petrol.

Of course the drinkers and smokers and travellers objected to this because it hit them in the hip-pocket. These people spoke out. One of them said the nation was striving for strength through misery. Others, too, had their say, with arguments based on wider considerations.

Letters, Gwen Smith. It is the same old story, told over and over again. Inflation comes, and the government raises taxes on some goods, and forces the prices up. That means that wages will have to increase, and that means that inflation will grow again, and so on.

Add to that the fact that the parliamentarians always give themselves pay rises, and so their minions get a rise, and soon the whole Public Service follows, and so everyone else gets one too. So we get more inflation.

The first thing our leaders should do, and that includes the men at the top of private corporations, is declare that **they will not be taking a pay rise for years**. Then we will see the inflation rate drop right away.

Letters, E J Gaffey. While one is inclined to applaud the action of the Government in taking positive steps in an attempt to arrest the inflationary trends of the Australian economy, it is a pity that such action leaves the consuming public open to exploitation by some unscrupulous retail traders.

Many traders have increased their prices within hours of the Prime Minister's announcement.

An intelligent analysis reveals the necessity for the increased taxation. But higher prices for the increase of retail traders' profit margins are not acceptable and should not be tolerated.

Letters, A Paoletti. In your recent editorials, you seem very concerned about the inflationary value of the migrant. On March 16 you stated, it is generally believed that the migrant costs the country something between 2,000 Pounds and 3,000 Pounds and can worsen trade balances by as much as 600 Pounds.

However, you fail to take into account some very important factors. First, the migrant begins to produce immediately he arrives in the country. Within the first year he may well produce to the value of 1,000 Pounds or more, so that within a few years he may have more than repaid the initial costs.

Secondly, and more importantly, each migrant over 21 represents an invested capital of more than 10,000 Pounds. It costs that sum and more to feed, clothe, educate and train **a person until his twenty-first year**. This capital has been invested in the country of origin of the migrant and **is being invested in Australia, free of charge**.

If the arrival of each migrant costs 2,000 Pounds or 3,000 Pounds then such a sum against a capital gift of 10,000 Pounds **leaves Australia richer by at least 7,000 Pounds**.

Letters, Peter Davey. I think that Mr Menzies has lost touch with the people. Surely he knows that raising the price of cigarettes and liquor and petrol will cause only a temporary dent in consumption. After a few weeks of sulking, every one will go back to normal.

I think that what Mr Menzies is trying to do is to teach the population the good values of Protestantism. Get the sinners away from booze and smoking and fast cars for a few weeks, and they will realise the errors of their ways, and flock back to the churches. He is not trying to cure inflation, but is instead recruiting for the churches he so loves to parade in.

Letters, F W Kaltenbach. Is there anybody who would say consumer spending should be maintained at an excessive rate while, through lack of funds, we cut down the States' building of homes, flood-control dams, schools, hospitals, roads, railways, power-houses, and placing of ex-Servicemen on farms?

These are the kinds of solid investments, essential for our development, to which money will be diverted that would otherwise be spent on consumer goods, many of them unessential, some of them pure luxuries.

I commend Mr Menzies for thus taking the unpopular anti-inflationary step of financing important works from revenue, instead of from the issue of Treasury bills and the contribution of moneys by the Commonwealth Bank, the Commonwealth sinking Fund, and other Federal Government agencies.

Comment. You can see that there is a mixed bag of responses. **And his cuts did in fact work.** The criticism remained, and was cited for years, that it would have been better if the Government had done something to create new businesses, or boost the overseas trading for existing old ones. That is, back to the argument in the intro above, it might well have stimulated the economy as well.

A NOTE ON HYGIENE

Here is a quaint practice that I am afraid was widespread.

Letters, C A G. Cannot something be done to discourage the disgusting habit of some bus and tram conductors in covering their fingers with their own saliva before pulling tickets for passengers? At one time, conductors were supplied with sponges. Has some union outlawed these as too hygienic?

OUR WHALING INDUSTRY

The Federal Government will sell the **Australian Whaling Commission's station at Carnarvon in northwest Western Australia**. The sale will be to the Nor'west Whaling Company. The new owners will continue to operate the station.

The Minister for Trade, in announcing the sale, reassured the public that the new owner will operate the station in the normal manner, and that he was confident that **it will continue to make a profit as in the past.**

APRIL NEWS ITEMS

A zebu steer escaped from its enclosure at **the Sydney Royal Easter Show**. **It charged though the crowd** followed by two stockmen on horses and was ultimately cornered and corralled when it became stuck in a narrow gateway. **50 people were injured, and 18 were taken to hospital by 10 ambulances.** During the chase, a constable fired a shot at the zebu, but he missed.

The Federal Minister for Supply announced that **preparations for the testing of atomic weapons at Monte Bello Islands** were going according to schedule. The test site is off the north west of Australia, and **British atomic agencies will take the lead role in the tests**. The first tests at this site were conducted in 1952.

Residents and surfers of Sydney living near **the mainstream beaches** are up in arms over **various proposals to mine rutile** from the beaches. They claim that the sites will be damaged by removal of the heavy rutile, which they claim, stabilises the sand. **Cash-hungry Councils** would like to get hold **of the royalties they would be paid. The battles rage on.**

Louis Armstrong, Satchmo, flew quietly into Sydney airport. Since he was here a year ago, **he has reduced his weight from 19 stone to 11 stone**. It helps him play his trumpet better. He said he had decided that his Australian tour was so important to him that he had not attended Princess Grace's Monaco wedding. He will play "*Mack the Knife*" at all concerts.

NSW will be the only State to charge for injections of the Salk anti-polio vaccine to children. Parents will be charged two shillings for each of three injections to each child.

April 8th. **Four crocodile eggs hatched in a TAA flight** from Townsville to Brisbane yesterday. **They were in a cardboard box in an Adelaide man's hand luggage.** With the crocodiles were four unhatched eggs, a two-foot lizard, and a seven-foot python....

The passenger **offered to keep the crocodiles in his shirt** for the rest of the trip "so they won't annoy the other passengers". But TAA insisted that the babies be off-loaded into a freight plane.

Sir Eugene Goossens resigned from his posts as conductor of the Sydney Symphony Orchestra and as director of the NSW Conservatorium of Music.

Clashes in the Middle East and between Egypt and Israel were becoming more frequent, and more serious. All the Big Powers were talking about intervening, and no one at all was listening to anyone.

April 17th. Actress Grace Kelly and Prince Rainier III of Monaco were married in a civil ceremony today. They will be re-married tomorrow in a Church wedding. The occasions will be marked by as much splendour as you would expect.

The **biggest shark ever caught in Sydney** was landed by a member of the Sydney Game Fishing Club. It weighed 2,100 pounds (nearly a ton), and was **16 feet in length**.

ANZAC DAY SPLITS RELIGIOUS GROUPS

For decades, Anzac marches in the cities, suburbs and towns round the nation had celebrated by having our ex-servicemen parade through the streets to some gathering point, and then having some form of religious service to honour the dead. There, they gave thanks for the survivors' deliverance from the hands of enemies. Many of the ex-servicemen who attended this service were not at all religious, but accepted the service for what is was. Namely, a brief moment where people were united in a common bond, and remembered the many thoughts, and the people, that had once been so precious to them.

To virtually everyone in the nation, at this precious moment, there was no suggestion that rivalries between religions had a place in the ceremony. So, **it came as a shock** when the NSW RSL Executive issued a statement that the main march in Sydney would end in a service from which **all clergy would be excluded**. Until now, such services had been conducted by mainly Protestant clergy.

This reflected the balance of religious denominations in the population. Most of the clergy had the good sense to be as non-denominational as possible, but it was inevitable that certain prayers would be said and hymns be sung that were foreign to Catholics in particular. Still, these latter accepted that the services were not part of a cunning plot to recruit new members, but simply an expression of an urgent need to remember all of those who had sacrificed so much.

From late-March, the barrage of Letters protesting this RSL decision was unrelenting. Almost every day for a month, two or three Letters a day were published in the *SMH.* Initially, this Letter from March 27 set the scene.

Letters, W G Hilliard, Bishop, St John's Rectory, Parramatta. If my information is correct, the proposed service which will be **acceptable to no denomination.** We are all anxious that the fallen comrades of the ex-Servicemen should be fittingly honoured, but **we also desire that Almighty God should be fittingly honoured**, and we question further whether a ceremony which deliberately removes the traditional religious service is a fitting honouring of the multitudes of Servicemen who devoutly served and worshiped God.

If other Churches, **notably the Catholic**, cannot accept the Protestant prayers that a combined service uses, and if they cannot acknowledge God in company with other Christians, **they could surely withdraw to their Cathedral nearby** without the rest of the community being deprived on such an occasion of the privilege of uniting in the public recognition of that God on whom, in the last resort, the national welfare rests and to whom we owe all the blessings we enjoy.

After that, the argument diverted all over the place. For example, some Catholics suddenly remembered that the Church forbade Catholics to partake of non-Catholic services. So, the realisation was that for forty years they had been doing the wrong thing.

Other arguments emerged. How could a so-called Christian service be conducted without the duly-appointed minister of God? Were not these latter the conduit through which God acted? How could such services be held if God did not get a single mention? Would a similar edict be also applied to the Dawn Service? Surely **there** at least the clergy should lead. But which clergy?

Then there were others who wrote that the purpose of the gathering was to remember the dead and the suffering of others, and the families, and had nothing to do with the God who had allowed it all to happen. Some writers said they wanted the Air Force to leave the march at a certain point, and go off to their own religious service.

I cannot cover all the themes that emerged. Below, though, I give you a sample of what was written..

Letters, A W Stephenson, President, Churches of Christ, Sydney. Churches of Christ urge the RSL to reconsider the decision to abandon the combined religious Anzac Day service in which the sacrifices of the nation are remembered.

Unitedly this nation stood together in the days of crisis, why should we not now join unitedly in asking God to bless those who have suffered?

Is the day coming when we will not be able to sing together: "God save the Queen?"

Letters, Thos Agst, United Protestant Assn, Sydney. It is regrettable that the Roman Catholic Church has **combined with Communists and atheists** to remove from our combined Anzac Day celebrations the religious portion of the service which has been in operation for the past 40 years. This is a time when professing Christian Churches should forget their "pinpricking" differences and get together for the general good of the community to save what is left of pure Christianity.

Letters, Bertha Mac Smith, Past National President, CWA of Australia. Why, at a time when the world is in such dire need of the strength that can only come from the Almighty, should what was originally a deeply religious service be changed into something purely secular? Are the children growing up to think of Anzac as something quite apart from God?

Letters, Thos Agst, United Protestant Association. In reply to E N Browne, I would say that while Roman Catholic priests attend public celebrations as representing the only true Church of Jesus Christ, Protestants are perfectly justified in protesting against what is suggested. When, however, Roman Catholic priests are prepared to associate with Protestant ministers and participate in public prayer and Bible reading on an equal footing, there will be no protests from the Protestant community. **The remedy rests with the Roman Catholic Church.**

Letters, A Catholic, Maitland. Some of the Protestant leaders have asked why Catholic ex-Servicemen should not pray together with their Protestant counterparts. After all they fought together – why not pray together?

In actual fact these people have lost sight of the fact that, whilst they fought together, **even then they did not pray together.**

There were other opinions. Here is one that supported the RSL's action.

Letters, Edith Haynesay. Having lived with my aunt and uncle, Dame Mary and the late **Mr W M Hughes**, for more than a quarter of a century, I feel that I should express views which I know would have their concurrence.

The Little Digger, in all his long and strenuous political life, held a strong faith, and it was always felt in the household that the service which concluded the march was a fitting tribute to Almighty God as honour to the fallen, and gratitude for those preserved.

Comment. This whole episode was a very unseemly display of sectarianism. As it unfolded, more and more ordinary people were affronted that such a display of intolerance, especially among the clergy, should interfere with what they regarded as a ceremony to honour the dead and living people who had served this nation so well.

Letters, Mrs D Van Gelder. What is all this nonsense about the Anzac Day service?

This should be at least one day in the year when people forget the differences in their many religions, and join together in a short commemoration to the memory of those who gave their lives so that all of us living today may enjoy the existence they were robbed of.

If the RSL is in such a hurry to start the "reunions" that it cannot spare the time for this short service for their own dead mates, then I cannot spare the time out of my busy life to **trudge round selling tin hats**, as I have done since I came to this little town in 1941.

I look on the RSL's action in this matter as an insult to my own war dead – my husband and my brother, who gave their lives in World War II.

Letters, Alan E Begbie, Senior Chaplain (CE). Who informed Mr Alexander that the "mass of members" in the RSL want the suggested change? At a recent meeting of our large and active branch, **a motion deploring the change received a unanimous vote** from members present, with one lone exception.

I, with countless others, would seek to stamp out the "ugly hand of sectarianism" wherever it may be thrust forward, but ask only for that form of service accepted for 40 years past: undenominational, and including only that in which every Christian should be able to take part.

On the day of the March, two services were held in Sydney. 50,000 people attended Hyde Park, and 20,000 massed in the Domain. It was remarked by many marchers that it was sad to see that **many Diggers who had fought side by side were forced to split up and go to different venues**. Many also said that it was important that such a divisive system would not survive into next year, and that some way could be found that would keep the community of Christians together, rather than split it.

LOTTERIES IN THE NEWS

For years, the NSW lottery had plodded along. Initially, when it was set up by the State Government, it was specified that all profit gained would be spent on hospitals. It had continued on in a non-spectacular manner anxious to keep a low profile lest anyone challenge just how much was indeed going to hospitals, and how much was going to Consolidated Revenue.

Victoria had over the last few years increased its lottery prizes, and now Tasmania was forcing the issue, with one recent prize of 500,000 Pounds. This compared with the NSW first prize of 12,000 Pounds. So, pressure was growing within NSW and elsewhere to follow the Tasmanian example.

Not everyone agreed that this should happen.

Letters, R E Eagar. I wish to protest against the increasing growth of the Tasmanian lottery.

This new lottery, with its very attractive bait of 500,000 Pounds, is sure to hook thousands upon thousands of gullible people – gullible because these organisers, with their tremendous advertising and publicity, play upon the fact that there are, in Australia, people who always seek that elusive pot of gold underneath the rainbow, no matter if they lay out Pounds and Pounds in the search.

As I see it, the special lottery in New South Wales, with its prize of 12,000 Pounds, is more than adequate as a prize.

Let people have their lotteries, but allow the cost of tickets to be within easy reach of the buyer with more smaller prizes, which I would expect to satisfy the vast majority of buyers.

NSW was also trying to raise its own revenue through marketing efforts that again weren't always appreciated by everyone.

Letters, R R Bruce. I was amazed to receive from Mr C T Tallentire, the Director of State Lotteries, a circular letter addressed "Dear Friend," drawing my attention to the fact that "very many, very busy people cannot afford the time to secure tickets in the New South Wales State Lotteries" and suggesting that **I establish an account with the Lottery Office** by forwarding a bank draft, money order, or cheque which could be applied as I direct towards the purchase of tickets weekly or monthly as the case may be in mammoth, special, or ordinary lotteries.

In nearly 25 years' experience as a solicitor I have received numerous requests for donations. I can safely say that every one of these requests has had considerable merit, but this last request takes its lonely place as an instance of brazen effrontery and a cynical indifference to the moral well-being of **a State already suffering from a plethora of gambling and alcohol**.

Mention of this letter suggests a similarity between Mr Tallentire's bright idea and that of the outback publican of past days who took the shearer's cheque and boots and let him "cut it out." Mr Tallentire literally wants my cheque (which he is not getting) and metaphorically asks for my shirt (which he is not getting either).

It is no use Mr Tallentire suggesting that his cause is a worthy one in so far as lottery moneys are applied to the upkeep of hospitals. Part of these moneys may be so applied, but generally speaking the State Lottery is regarded by the Government as an income-producing institution whose funds should find their way into the general revenue.

Meanwhile, most States were considering the proposition that they could gain revenue by running special lotteries, with big prizes and expensive ticket prices, and cloak their profit-making **under the flag of the Olympic Games**. Part of this cunning device was to say that part of the profits would go to some aspect of sponsoring the Games. Surely, such a patriotic promise could raise no objections.

Well, don't be too sure.

Letters, M D Finlay. It is reported that Mr Arthur Drysdale will give an undisclosed amount from his 10 per cent profit in the forthcoming Tasmanian "super mammoth" Olympic Games lottery to the Australian Olympic Federation. Present at this announcement were the Federation's secretary, Mr Edgar Tanner, and the Federation's executive office, Mr W Uren.

Is the attitude of the Australian Olympic Games Federation in supporting **the business of a professional lottery organiser is in the interests of amateur sport?**

The Olympic champions of ancient Greece were rewarded not by prizes, but with a simple wreath of olive leaves. And once the organisation of those ancient Games became allied with outside commercial interests, as they did in the time of the Roman Emperor Nero, then they lost their true spirit and the Olympic flame died out.

Both Messrs Tanner and Uren have done much for amateur sport in this country. But I suggest that they and their fellow-officers of the Australian Olympic Federation would be doing a service neither to that Federation nor to the spirit of the Olympic Games if they persist in their active support of this professionally organised, profit-making, gambling organisation.

Comment. One thing I have learned while writing these books is that there are at least two sides to every argument. In fact, most often, there are sometimes up to a dozen sides to a decent argument.

Given that insight, I was not surprised to find that next day, there was the following rejoinder.

Letters, John T Bryden-Brown. There is no doubt that the whole success of the modern Olympic Games depends on the retention of the spirit of the ancient games on which they are based. However, conditions of today and of thousands of years ago are vastly different.

The competing world is very much larger, the number of competitors would probably exceed the audience watching the Games in those days, and the organisation and cost would be vastly greater. Therefore, any assistance the Olympic Games Federation receives should be welcomed, and there is no wonder that Messrs Tanner and Uren were grateful to receive the biggest donation ever presented by a private individual – the donation from Mr Drysdale, of Tasmanian Lotteries.

Where there is little objection to the proceeds of lotteries being devoted to hospitals and other social services as they are in most States, including Tasmania, surely there can be no objection for the proceeds being used to help such a vital thing as our Olympic Games.

In view of these facts, surely Mr Finlay's remarks are not warranted, and surely Mr Drysdale's example could be followed by other business organisations, and individuals interested in the successful promotion of the Games.

Comment. One development of the last sixty years has been the rise and rise of legalised gambling, sanctioned by the States, all of whom now depend on gambling to balance their budgets. Beginning with the TABs, and then the pokies, and concluding with Lottos and on-line betting, and the like, the growth has been spectacular. Of course, there has been much opposition at times, such as the moves to limit the effects of poker machines, but it seems that in general, from the volume of money changing hands, **that the public are not too upset by all this**. Though, I suspect, that if I pressed this point too hard here, **my Inwards Mail folder would get quite a fillip**.

AUSTRALIAN AUTHORS

Books written by Oz authors were never on the local lists of best-sellers. A few writers were popular and well-known, but the vast majority were indeed struggling. Some of them complained that when they went to public libraries, they watched borrowers, and noticed that as they browsed the shelves, when they got to Australian authors, they simply walked past. Some of the others said that if they had a good book ready for publication, they sent it overseas, sometimes with a flash false name.

This rather damning Letter seemed to reflect what many agreed was the current status of our writing.

Letters, H G Morgan. I note with regret your advocacy in your leading article of the plan to establish a Chair in Australian Literature. I can see no justification for the expenditure of such a sum as 80,000 Pounds on a project which smacks so much of petty nationalism. The truth is that most of **the writings of Australians are not great literature**. Indeed, the standard is so poor that very few, if any, works by Australian writers are well known outside this country. **Why then a Chair to study the second-rate?**

For Professor Milgate to claim that "Australian literature has a status and a quality worthy of academic recommendation" seems to me unjustifiable. Any such status exists only in the minds of the authors themselves and their more provincial-minded supporters.

Yet all was not lost. The quiet words of an American friend offered us hope for the future.

Letters, John Greenway, Professor, University of Denver, Colorado. On my arrival in Sydney several weeks ago to study Australian folk-songs, I was astonished to learn that there was no Chair of Australian literature at the universities.

I assumed that this lack was due to economic expediency, but after reading Mr Morgan's letter to the "Herald", I see that there actually is opposition to such a chair on the intellectual level.

As a teacher of American literature, let me warn that the arguments propounded by Mr Morgan precisely echo those which opposed the native American literature 100 years ago. Of course Australian literature is "second-rate" when judged against the standards of a culture which it imitates at present; but Australian literature has an incipient vitality that must eventually supersede that of the mother country.

Certainly it must be apparent to Mr Morgan that in attacking the "provincial-minded" and tacitly suggesting the perpetuation of a stultifying colonial attitude, he is advocating a policy of cultural sterility. If Australia is ever to establish itself as a nation in the fullest sense of that term, it must recognise and respect its own potentialities.

I hope that Australians will pardon this intrusion of an American into a national controversy, but it seems to me that if the United States Government considers Australian literature of sufficient quality to send students 7,000 miles to study it, surely Australians ought to value it no less highly.

Comment. His words were prophetic. Once we threw off the limitations imposed by the pretentions of literature in England, and once we realised that **a book and literature have little in common,** Australian authors have thrived.

SMOKE GETS IN THE EYES

Police in NSW have revealed that **a pointless swindle** has been plaguing the population for two years. Rumours are spread in a township that collectors of 3,000 empty Craven A cigarette packets will be given a cash **grant** for the local hospital, or of a wheelchair for the Spastic Centre....

The **cigarette makers state that this is not true**, but country towns are still forming well-meaning groups who parade the streets and clubs looking for discarded packets.

MAY NEWS ITEMS

The Commonwealth Bank is offering **a reward of 1,000 Pounds** for information leading to the conviction of the person or persons who are **distributing counterfeit forged 5 Pound notes in Melbourne.** 255 such notes have been detected in the last three weeks. **Any notes found will be confiscated** and the innocent holders will **not** be compensated.

Australia beware. A new word is coming into our language. **In Britain, strikes are occurring because employers are introducing "automation".** Larger machines will replace lots of smaller ones, and will require less manpower. **The push-button economy is about to arrive**, wherein production lines of workers will be replaced by intelligent machines with "brains".

Melbourne, feeling jealous of Sydney that a zebu bull had stolen the nation's headlines last month, **staged its own bit of rodeo. "600 pounds of maddened bullock"** brought an hour of terror to the streets of the West Footscray suburb at lunch-time yesterday. The bullock chased two women and a man, aged 82, it rammed a truck and charged two children as the mother watched screaming. **Finally it was shot dead by a man from a nearby factory.**

The City of Sydney is about to see its first parking meters. 145 meters will be installed **in the centre of the city**. This will create different traffic flows and at least **five fruit barrows will have their licences cancelled.**

A nation-wide shearers strike has been going on for a month, and shows no sign of ending. The rate of pay for shearers has been cut in line with the international fall in the price of wool, but the shearers refuse to accept the new Award. They are declaring "black" any property that uses non-union **Labor** to shear. This is causing **many ugly disputes** right across the nation.

May 17th. British scientists **exploded a "small" atomic weapon yesterday in the Monte Bello Islands**, off the coast of Western Australia.

In NSW, **poker machines are illegal in clubs. This law is not enforced** in social clubs if the revenue from the machines is seen to be improving members' amenities....

The ULVA is an association that looks **after brewers' interests.** It will soon begin various Court actions that would, if successful, **remove the licences from clubs that use poker machines**. The reason is that **revenue that should be going to beer sales is now going into the machines. And of course, we can't have that.**

The Australian cricket team is starting a tour of England. This week, **it lost a three-day match against county team Leeds.** This is the first time that Australia **has lost to a county side since 1912.**

The shearers' strike took a new twist today when the wharfies refused to load "black" wool into ships.

Sir Eugene Goossens left Australia for Rome on May 27th. **His family said that he will never return.** They were bitter about the actions that had led to his resigning from his posts.

US INFLUENCE ON AUSTRALIA

The *SMH* journalist, Gavin Souter, wrote a three-stage article on the new influence of the US in Australia since the War. He noted all the obvious things like popular songs, comic books, self-service stores, baseball and canasta. Australians attend square dancing, fly fox tails from their car aerials, and drop the "u" from words like "honour". They wear baseball caps and jeans, chew gum, and dance to juke boxes. They watch US films and movie cartoons and travelogues and serials. This list goes on and on, and is growing.

At a different level, US books have permeated our reading. Mickey Spillane dominates crime, and Zane Grey introduced us to the Wild West. Perry Mason fills our law courts. Our imports from America have grown and they include tons of cars and machinery, and more tons of US cigarettes. All of this means a corresponding fall in the influence of Britain, despite our population remaining based on Britain, and the majority of our migrants coming from there.

American experts are in demand in art galleries, for info about frogs, oil, hospital administration, libraries, orchids, and juvenile delinquency. We send our own experts to the US to learn about such matters as coalmining, groceries, music, tuberculosis, and dentistry.

Souter says that given all these apparent influences, many serious thinkers are surprised that Australia has not become more American. For example, we have kept our Australian accent. Souter concludes by reassuring us that it seems to him, after studying this process, that it will only go so far, and that we are not likely to become the Yankeeland beneath the Southern Cross. He expects we will simply gradually assimilate material from **both** Britain and America, and put them together to grow our own national identity.

The first Letter of alarm was from Australian cartoonist, Emile Mercier, one of our best-known cartoonists ever.

He writes that the article, *Tug o' War for The Australian Way of Life*, talks about the Americanisation of Australia, and invites responses on what can be done about it.

Firstly, he says, that he fully agrees with the *SMH*. All our music and movies are dominated by American interests, and so too is our radio. Press reports fit into the same category. This is particularly disturbing to journalists who can see how the situation is developing at a fast rate.

In his own case, he is an artist and cartoonist with 30 years' experience, and finds it regrettable that preference is given to overseas art work in any form, and of course particularly to comic strips.

Mercier goes on to say that in this case, about 100 per cent of **comics** are imported to Australia. He conjures up the vision of an American tourist looking at a newsstand and seeing nothing but American comic strip characters and then looking at a paper and seeing the same. Then he looks at our movies, and again can see only Hollywood products. What impression does he get about Australia's artistic achievements and national character? Surely this is the wrong impression.

Mercier then goes on to answer what can be done about it. He urges Prime Minister Menzies to "put the pruning knife through some of the imbecile comic strips" or to place tariffs on them.

Other writers had their say.

Letters, E K White. I read Gavin Souter's articles on American influence in Australia with great interest.

Apart from purely academic questions, the overriding consideration for Australia must be our security and survival.

Inevitably, a nation of 160-odd million people must make an impact on one of 10 million. There is much that we can learn and appreciate from America. While the basic pattern of our way of life follows that of Great Britain, we can only benefit by absorbing the best that the US has to offer, and accepting that country's generous friendship and co-operation, which we surely need if we are to survive.

Mr Souter did not touch on what to me seems a vital point – that friendship with the US, and emulation of some US practices and habits, do not connote a weakening of our British ties. It implies rather a realisation of geographical and political changes developing from common interests in the Pacific, and a desire, by friendship and co-operation, to strengthen and preserve the Commonwealth.

It is important to realise and remember that Australia must shoulder the responsibility for holding and developing this great country. In doing so, we should welcome friendship with Britain **and** America, but should aim to build a truly Australian character. We can do that best by absorbing **all** that is good from outside, and rejecting the dross.

Letters, Duncan MacCallum. The United Kingdom has, of course, changed over the years with growing urban and popular – and American – influences. But we can to our benefit still find **there** something of calm and of quality and of compromise that is not so obviously imported from across the Pacific.

Letters, (Mrs) E Coram. Apropos of the question as to whether we are getting too Americanised, I (as a third generation Australian of British stock) say "Why not?"

When one wants to learn anything, one should go to the best teacher and, as I see it, Australia is a country very much like America geographically (only upside down). Our stage of development is about par with America 100 years ago, therefore, if we keep following in her footsteps, by the time we have 160 million people here, we will be as efficiently and fully developed a country as she is today, and who can ask for more.

I say it is a pity more countries were not more Americanised.

Letters, B T C. Since my arrival in Australia I have been just amazed at the determination of Australians to identify themselves with America and the Americans.

The fact that 85 per cent of recordings heard in Australia are American in both origin and technique, does not do much credit to Australia, but merely increases the impression, of the desire to imitate, and serves to demonstrate how unlike Americans are the Australians in originality.

The most fantastic claim heard to date must surely be that both historically and geographically, Australia and America are alike. As one who has travelled extensively in America and quite widely in Australia, I find them singularly unalike in both aspects.

How could anyone possibly **compare a country as incredible as America**, a country that is the most prosperous and powerful of all time, and a people undeniably the most catered for in the world, in fact a phenomenon, and the wonder of the modern age, **with a country boasting no metropolis**, but a series of dreary provincial cities with dull buildings, mediocre stores, holiday resorts where it is almost impossible to find restaurants wholesome enough to eat in, and where even though on holiday, there is nothing to do and nowhere to go after nightfall?

What a great pity that Australia will probably be known as the country that tried (without very much success) to emulate America.

The only future I see for **Sydney is that it will just get bigger and drearier**, and **its inhabitants more complacent and smug** in their erroneous belief that they are like the Americans, so much so that they find it unbelievable that it is not the desire of everyone to live here.

Letters, W Kehor. I am an American. I have been here one year and I have been amazed at the intensity of the American influence in Australia.

In advertising, especially, there is a constant attempt to label the article being publicised as "American." As a rule the items which are sold with all this ballyhoo have little, if any, resemblance to the thing imitated.

As a result, the discriminating Australian, who is not familiar with the US original, has a very poor impression of it. This is bad for good international understanding since the US has something more to export than cheap gadgets.

Of course the most pervasive influence is a kind of social conditioning which results from the popularity of Hollywood films and American entertainers on the radio and on records. The prevalence and preference for American entertainment at every level, including the legitimate theatre (usually featuring American plays), has really surprised me. This affects fashions of dress and some patterns of speech and behaviour, but I think, does not go much deeper.

In fact, I am of the opinion that the dreaded influence is quite superficial and I am aware of very fundamental differences between Australians and Americans which I hope will continue to exist and which I classify as follows:

Lack of American competitive spirit due to small population and large opportunities (Result: Fewer ulcers and less coronary thrombosis).

Lack of materialistic outlook, probably stemming from the same reasons (Result: Better adjusted, more carefree and congenial outlook with a healthy interest in sport).

On the other hand, Australians seem to me much more willing to be told what to do and to obey rules and regulations without protest. They also seem much more regimented in their thinking and custom-bound. They are obviously inimical to change. I think this is regrettable.

Two other writers expressed the opinion that the American influence was as yet superficial. One, a clergyman said that it was to be found only in Sydney. Another went a bit further and said "Sydney is not Australia, and in spite of comic-strips, Hollywood and jazz, one has only to go west to find the real Australia, which resembles Sydney about as much as Hollywood resembles the Mid-West States of America."

Comment. The Editor, perhaps wisely, closed Letters at this stage. He might have been deluged by Letters protesting against advice from our American friends.

In any case, in 2016, I think that the nation is even more **international** than anyone thought it would be. Let me illustrate with a few trivial examples. Apple has a big share of the mobile phone market, **but so too** does Samsung and its Asian colleagues. PC's now come mainly from Asia.

American Yank Tanks have gone and so too have their other gas guzzlers. Yet we take a lot of US movies and computer-ware, and we cooperate on Defence. Yet again, our own **local** pop music and movie industries are doing well.

My point is that we are influenced by many different cultures, and it is hard to see any single one dominating.

WHO IS AN AMATEUR SPORTSMAN?

With the Olympics coming up, the question that was being asked was just who is an **amateur** sportsman. This was important because all competitors in the Games were supposed to be amateurs. Professionals were not allowed.

This was a vexing question for a lot of sportsmen. There were no doubts in golf, for example. All the major golf competitions were primarily for professionals, but amateurs were welcome. Rugby League had no restrictions on being paid a bonus for a win, or a steady retainer. Tennis had its pros and amateurs, but these were not allowed to play together. Rugby Union had no pros at all. Jockeys were paid for every ride. So it was a mixed picture across the different sports.

But it was not as simple as that. The picture was changing rapidly. For example, in some sports and clubs that were not supposed to give payments to players, surely it was proper to **pay their expenses**. Maybe actual costs that could be receipted, or maybe a daily away-from-home allowance. Perhaps these **could be generous**, and maybe do more than cover basic expenses.

Or maybe for international trips, say, the athlete could travel first-class. Surely it was good policy to get an athlete somewhere in the world in good health and condition. If so, does that not mean first-class travel? And then, three days of recuperation in foreign climes after the event.

Then there was the issue of publicity. The **images** of sportsmen were starting to appear everywhere, and their **endorsements** of various products were becoming important to advertisers. The rules were pretty clear that Olympic athletes could not accept money for appearing on cigarette ads or washing machine ads, but could they not be paid by other means? Could money be paid to the local Clubs that sponsored them? Could the advertisers pay for the extra training that the Club arranged for the athletes? Could money be found to enable travel to events that were normally too costly to attend? There was a myriad of ways of skinning this cat, and the number of them was growing rapidly.

I give you below a mixed bag of Letters that this issue provoked. Some relate to the Olympics, some do not. But they all point to the changes that lay ahead, and to the diminishing role that amateurism would play in sport.

Letters, Allan Richards. No one in this country would wish to see our distinguished athletes indiscriminately recommending somebody's cigarettes or someone else's toothpaste, but in the case under review it appears that no such commercialisation is involved.

The autograph seekers and souvenir collectors are found in every sports gathering; it is they who support amateur sport and make it possible for any country to raise a team of champions.

One must expect that the next few months, badges, photographs and other souvenirs of our athletes will make their appearance in the stores, as is the case in every other country which stages the Olympic Games. If commercial firms, who are best able to sponsor such publicity, are forbidden to do this, then it is going to be a poor show for Australian sportsmen.

It is quite wrong to suppose that these athletes do not need or want publicity. In many cases, that is the only tangible benefit they derive from their strenuous efforts. Competitive sport today is a hard and grueling business involving tremendous sacrifices in time and leisure, and the more publicity that is accorded to the amateur the better.

If a manufacturer sees fit to spend his money publicising the exploits of his country's athletes and does it in a proper and dignified manner, so much the better.

Letters, R Stirling. In Australia, we are perhaps somewhat slow to appreciate the value of publicity of every kind to a young man or woman about to embark on a career. Now that we are about to stage the greatest sports show in the world, it is high time for us to alter that view.

Standards in publicity and showmanship are continually changing, and what may have been appropriate at the Berlin Games in 1936 will be lost completely in 1956. Let us not overlook the fact that it is the athletes themselves who are the ones chiefly concerned, not the officials.

Big commercial firms can well afford to give a helping hand to these boys and girls, and I hope they will do so by publicising their efforts and achievements.

Comment. Both of these Letters like the idea of Olympic athletes getting **the publicity** from advertising. Perhaps it would be good for the image of a young person, and that might stand him well in the future. But neither of them dared to say that most, if not all, of the athletes, were as human as the rest of us, and **wanted something more tangible than publicity**. There is no doubt that they got it.

Letters, Walter Sternberg, Hakoah Soccer Football Club. In the article "Soccer Gets a Shot in the Arm", the Hakoah Soccer Club is referred to as a "wealthy Jewish concern". It is true that Hakoah is a Jewish club as far as its membership and most of its registered players are concerned, but it is neither "wealthy" (to our regret) nor is it a "concern," a term that implies a business or a company. It is run as businesslike as honorary officials can manage for a spare-time hobby.

Financially, Hakoah, like most other amateur sporting bodies, must depend on gate receipts and membership subscriptions, and no doubt our financial position is inferior to that of other leading Soccer clubs in NSW.

The most serious inaccuracy however, is the allegation that Hakoah is paying certain named players "big weekly retainers." This statement is false. Not a single Hakoah player is paid to play Soccer. Furthermore, it would be in contravention of the constitution of the NSW Soccer Football Association, with which we are affiliated, to do so.

I might point out that officials and committee-members are excluded, serving on a wholly honorary basis.

Comment. Going back to the Olympics, I should mention that about this time, **nationalistic fervour was being deliberately manipulated** by the big nations **as part of the thrust and parry of the Cold War**. Russia and America both wanted to be seen as the saviours of the world, and this flowed over into the idea that they should be seen to be super-human at all things, including athletics. So, from about this date, both of these nations, and a few others, put much money into providing the best coaches, training fields, accommodation for athletes, uniforms, and glory that money could buy. Of course, the spirit of amateurism survived, but no one could say it came out lily white.

A GOOD DEED APPRECIATED

Here is this little gem from an American friend.

Letters, Alice G Robbins of Denver (Colorado). I want to tell you about an incident which took place in the hotel at which I am staying in Athens last night.

The lounge was full of guests just before dinner. There were people of seven nationalities to my knowledge – Greek, Italian, German, Spanish, British, American, Australian. Then a young, well-dressed American Negro came in the doorway. The hum of talk died abruptly and everyone stared at him. The silence was awful.

The Negro paused and was about to turn away when a man wearing a little badge of Australia on his lapel walked right across the lounge, with his hand outstretched, and up to the Negro. He shook hands with him, then took him back to where he had been sitting, with his hand on the Negro's shoulder, and had a drink with him.

It was such a spontaneous gentlemanly act that everyone clapped. It made Australia a lot of friends, because there was no doubt about what nationality the man was, owing to his badge. I found out he was Mr John Laffin, a writer from your country. It was the most wonderful thing I ever saw and it breaks my heart it wasn't an American who did it; the film star Danny Kaye was one of the Americans present. But no, it had to be an Australian. Now I know what I've heard about Australians is true.

There was a follow-up, in this plea for similar consideration for our own Aborigines.

Letters, J E H. Bravo for Mr John Laffin! Let us all rejoice that, at last, the true brotherhood of mankind is a matter of honest deeds and not mere lip-service to ideals.

Pray now that he will hasten home to these shores and initiate the first steps to holding an **all-Aboriginal party in the lounge of the Hotel Australia**.

A NEW MARKETING GIMMICK

The NSW Egg Marketing Board might introduce **shell-less eggs** into Australia. They are on sale in the US, and the Board is sending officers there to see what they offer here.

They are raw eggs in a transparent square-shaped plastic container. A buyer can see the yolks and whites before buying them. All that was necessary was to pull a tag on the container and lift off the top. This means you do not get gritty shell mixed with the egg. **The US study continues.**

BETTER RELATIONS WITH EGYPT?

Britain's friendship with Egypt has been strained recently as they squabble over who benefits from the Suez Canal. But in May, there were celebrations as **the British honoured their promise to hand over control of the Canal** to the Egyptians. The Egyptian President, Colonel Nasser, promised a future of co-operation with the British, US, and Russia.

JUNE NEWS ITEMS

A representative from the NSW rural parish of Scone attended a meeting of the Synod of the Church of England. He pleaded for **the church to bring single women from overseas to marry lonely migrants**. He claimed that at Scone there were 350 men who were **"the loneliest men in the world"**.

June 9th. **The wool dispute is getting serious.** The **black** wool is making its way back to the nation's ports, and union members are refusing to handle it. Then, for example, three large wool stores in Sydney have dismissed all their storemen and packers. **More and more unions are getting involved in the ban on the wool**, though some unions are abstaining. The situation is one of great confusion.

One for cricket-followers. In the First Test match in England, Australian bowlers Keith Miller and Ron Archer **bowled unchanged for an entire session of two hours**. **A feat unheard of 60 years later.**

June 12th. **The Labor Party is in a great mess nation-wide.** Last night, the Federal Executive in Melbourne ruled that **the entire NSW Executive was dismissed**. This is typical of the great battles that are being fought within the Party. One such battle is the fight **by the Roman Catholic so-called Groupers to reduce Red influence in the Party**. **This chaos will leave it impotent for another dozen years.**

In 1826, two convicts on a ticket-of-leave were farming near Campbelltown, near Sydney. Their names were

Fisher and Worrall. **On June 19th, a man shudderingly** walked into the Black Sheep Shanty, and announced that **he had just seen a ghost on the bridge, and that it bore the appearance of Fisher**. It was covered with blood, croaking like a frog, and pointing towards a swamp.,..

Investigations **found Fisher's body, covered in three feet of mud. He had been murdered with an axe.** Worrall was charged, found guilty and hanged....

News item, June 20th. A crowd of **400 people thronged the town bridge at midnight last night**. It was, however, disappointed, **as once again the famous Fisher's Ghost failed to appear.**

It was announced that **the play** Summer of the Seventeenth Doll **will be taken to London next year**. It had played to big audiences in Melbourne, Sydney and Brisbane over the last nine months, and had been a huge success. **An Australian cast will do the London performances**, and this will be an opportunity to put Australian plays on show in an international context, says **writer Ray Lawler**. An Australian stage-play showing in London is a rarity.

The Sutherland Council in Sydney voted **to introduce a tree-preservation order within residential areas**. It prohibited the ring-barking, topping, cutting down or destruction of any tree without Council permission. It is seeking advice from various quarters on whether the order will be legally enforceable. If so, it will be **the first Council to introduce such an order**.

PUBLIC TRANSPORT WOES

During the War, and in the next decade after that, this nation did not have the money to do much to fix its transport systems. This meant that there was virtually no spending on trams, buses and railways, and that roads and bridges and airports simply fell into disrepair. **After the War**, much money was spent on establishing a welfare state that provided some sort of monetary back-up for those unfortunate enough to need it, and **by 1956** there was a loud cry for national spending to relieve the long-term housing and rental problems.

So, **given all that**, and the tremendous distances that our trains and roads had to satisfy, it was little wonder that this nation was finding serious faults with all aspects of our transport system. Thus, over many months, **the papers were full of complaints**. This was not just confined to one city or State, but was instead widespread across the nation.

Take for example, the complaint about replacing trams in the centre of Sydney.

Letters, L A Clark. Your newspaper has consistently advocated the abolition of Sydney's trams and their replacement by buses. As recently as June 4, your sub-leader concluded with these words: "And the sooner the clogging trams can be replaced, the better it will be for transport generally."

To replace trams, means the purchase of more and more buses, all of which are imported. Most of the rubber and all the fuel and spare parts are also obtained from overseas, constituting a continuous and ever-increasing expenditure which contributes in no small way to our adverse trade balance.

Is it more important to remove trams from Sydney's streets or to conserve our overseas exchange for items which are necessary to the nation's economy?

Here the writer talks about issues as **she** saw them, and they might or might not have had some substance. But in all places across the nation, there were similar Letters urging some course of action about buses, and trains, and roads, and potholes, and marking on roads, and intersections, and bridges, and you name it. The point was that our infrastructure needed replacement, and that our politicians were concentrating on other matters, and there was no coherent lobby working to make this an urgent policy matter. This was a problem whose time had not yet come.

There were other nagging problems. The employees of the various authorities in that system were under constant attack. One criticism was that when they travelled to work, they did not pay fares. "Surely the transport workers travelling to work, and there are thousands of them, could pay their way or at least half of it." They were criticised for being inconsiderate or lazy. "Why is it that every second day, I wait on the tram for the conductor to come and collect my fare, but he never gets to me?" "Why can't the conductor wait a few seconds before he pulls the cord so that customers can sit down first? That is, if they can find a seat."

Then again they are "unfit for human observation. They are paid a dry-cleaning allowance to tidy up their uniforms once a month. This should be called a wet-cleaning allowance, because the only thing it is used for is to buy beer. Has any one ever seen a railway porter looking spick and span?" Given all these complaints about the personnel, the solution is obvious. "The Government should hand over all public transport to private enterprise. There would be no losses then and no slovenly workers either."

At about this time, State Governments were in the business of raising fares to cover their rising costs and increasing losses. This brought forth a large number of complaints.

Letters, G Oliver. On every previous occasion when fares have been raised, the deficit has got greater – and the reason is very easy to see. When the first section was 2d, I thought nothing of getting in a bus to do my daily shopping and coming home the same way. When the first section went to 4d, I walked both ways. Instead of gaining an extra 4d, the buses lost it.

Once, after a concert at the Town Hall, it was difficult to get a footing on a tram to Wynyard. Now the trams go down practically empty.

The Government should practise Henry Ford's method of bringing its commodity to the people. When he found he was not selling enough cars he reduced the price – and sold more.

Letters, Kerwin Maegraith. Extortionate fares are not the answer to the present transport mess. Any group of competent businessmen will tell you that to sell your product you have to charge a rate that is economical and fair. You also have to provide first-class service. I have solved the difficulty in my own way. I walk.

In our congested city, it is much quicker and more comfortable to walk. **Who prefers being hunted along the corridor** and told to "move along there" a dozen times in an overcrowded vehicle, **to sniffing the morning air** and using the muscles of the body as they should be used? My walking keeps me in first-class condition and, if the medical profession had to live on what they get from me, they would starve.

Letters, P V Heatherington. The most disturbing item in the list of fare and freight increases is the 10 per cent increase in freight on milk.

If this is passed on to the public, as it must necessarily be, it will mean a heavy penalty on families with young children, especially on the families in the lower wage groups.

Already the price of milk in NSW is too high, through no fault of the producers, and surely it is the business of the Government to see that this vital commodity is retailed at a price within the means of all?

Every effort should be made by the general public to have this freight increase - and, indeed, freights on all essential foodstuffs - reduced to the former level.

Letters, Colin M Rose. Instead of giving the public a 50 per cent burden, why not offer collectors a 5 per cent incentive over a certain quota to be collected? This might encourage the collection of those fares lost from people who are never asked or who travel a couple of sections before a conductor approaches.

Letters, H W Naylor. The limiting of population sprawl and consolidation of the city's growth, with **new and improved transport routes** as envisaged by the Cumberland County planning scheme, **is the city's only hope** of becoming a workable metropolis, and not a featureless scatter of paralysed units. The outer limit of urban growth laid down by the county plan must be rigidly adhered to until proper and intelligent re-development has taken place in the inner areas.

Letters, I Elliot Gilest. The higher transport rates will increase the cost of living, and there will be another outcry for higher wages and still more inflation, which has already destroyed two-thirds of the value of our money. It is indeed to be hoped that those responsible for this persistent madness will learn a little simple addition before they have entirely wrecked our economy. The public cannot have it both ways. If they ask for higher wages, they must pay for them.

In NSW, railway **freight rates** were also raised this month.

Finally, let me conclude this section with a Letter that will once again ring bells with long-distance train travellers.

Letters, (Mrs) J Friend. One certainly has to be strong and in very good health to withstand the rigours of the overnight train trip between Melbourne and Sydney.

My father, a man who has been retired for some years, arrived at Central at 9.15 on June 21, looking as though he had been through some grim ordeal. He was: (1) Gaunt from lack of sleep; (2) unshaven; (3) downright hungry.

The reason for his lack of sleep was that he was just too cold to sleep. The train travelled through a bitterly cold night, with thick frost lying like snow on the ground, yet there was no heating in his compartment – not even foot warmers. The consequence was that, when he went to bed, even though there were plenty of blankets, he just couldn't warm up all night.

The reason for his being unshaven was that there was no hot water – not even warm water – to have a wash on this cold winter's morning.

He was frankly hungry, because, although the train was not due into Central till 9.15a.m., there was no breakfast to be had.

If this is the way the railways treat their best paying customers, is it any wonder that those customers seek other means of travel?

All of this might remind some readers of cattle trains. But the complaints against real cattle trains were endless.

Without Laboring the point, they told of masses of cattle being forced into over-crowded railway trucks and carried hundreds of miles, standing for days at times, without food and water to the slaughter yards. A grim picture, repeated year after year.

Comment. This small collection of reports is only a sample of the mass of material that was written and published about public transport. The question that I ask now, more than half a century later, was how was it that such an obvious burning issue could go on for so long, for another thirty years and more, and not receive the attention it deserved? It is true that we have a huge country and a small population so that infrastructure and associated costs are very high here. Also, our population was spread thinly in all except a few capital cities. But even so, maybe more resources could have been put into transportation. Then again when I think about it, where could any such money come from? I suppose there is no easy answer. **What do you think?**

OUR PLACE IN ASIA

We all know that Australia is located down the bottom of the world, and that it is far from any real civilisation. Sadly, not only is it a long way from the centre of the universe, England, but it is cut off by all sorts of people, most of whom are of odd colours, and many of whom are scarcely civilised. If you travel from England as the crow flies, you pass through the murderous Balkans, the multitudes of swarming Indians, then across into the Asian nations with their suspicious war-records and abominable standards of living, and ignorance, and lack of culture, till you get to the Indonesians, who are all Muslims who want to colonise West New Guinea.

This little parody seems far fetched, and indeed to say that it represents a typical Australian's view of our place in the world **is really** stretching the point. Yet, in 1956, the good Aussie in the backyard at the Sunday barbie did have a collection of such views, all mixed up together with more sober and educated ideas.

So, now I will bring a few of these attitudes to your attention. But before I do, I should remind you that in the background of most people's mind was still the deep hatred and suspicion of the Japanese, emanating from the War. And, for many of us, to prove we were not discriminatory, some at least of this suspicion spilled over to **all** Asians.

First I will draw attention to the White Australia Policy. Basically this said that **Asians were not welcome** as permanent residents in Australia. It was still being enforced here, with only the very occasional exception. Mind you, **the Asian nations were not at all keen** on their white-skinned neighbours from Australia settling on **their** shores either. But their resistance was not highlighted by the so-called **White** Australia Policy. Had the Japanese announced a **Yellow** Japanese Policy, would **we** have grumbled as much as the Asians were always doing?

In any case, the first few Letters focus on our WAP.

Letters, L A Lambourne. It would be political suicide for any party to advocate the repeal of the 1901 Immigration Act, but at least the Government could adopt a policy of treating each case on its merits. In other words instead of laying down a dogmatic line, it would interpret the Act in such a manner as **to**

allow for certain exemptions. This would be truly a Christian approach to the problem of Asian migration.

This was the case when the Federal Government decided to allow a number of Japanese brides of Australian Servicemen to enter Australia, and this single act has given Australia a very good name in Japan. On Australia Day, most leading Japanese newspapers editorially praised us on this matter.

A similar problem could be found in Malaya where there are Australian troops. Great harm would be done if the Government refused to allow Malayan brides into this country.

For the time being, as the first step towards the repeal of this outdated policy, we should follow a humane approach in the interpretation of the Act. I believe that it will increase the friendship that exists today between Australia and Asia.

Letters, W E Bennett. The "White Australia Policy" may have been wise at the time. With the change of outlook that has come to the world, many may see wisdom in a change of outlook.

A quota system might be tried. We are getting many students from other countries here in Australia. These students might provide a suitable ground to draw from. The **pride of race and religion are becoming out of date** and we need a broad outlook.

Letters, Australia Alba. I regret your leading article, which, I think, had been better left unwritten.

If we allow a quota from any Asian country to enter Australia, then we should have to allow quotas from all Asian and African countries. I very much doubt our ability to control the numbers and quality of those entering, and, in any case, **why create a colour problem where none exists?** We have been left a wonderful heritage by our forefathers, and let us not have to say like Virginius, "What their care bequeathed us, our madness has flung away."

Letters, J J Carlton, Sydney University Liberal Club.
What would it cost us to make a change?

No one suggests that immigration is an answer to the over-population problem in Asia: all that is asked is that we admit a token number of immigrants to show that our immigration policy is not based on racial prejudice.

I would uphold most strongly our right to maintain Australia as a predominantly **British** nation, but this right is not challenged by the quota proposal. Nor does it challenge our economic security. **The fears expressed by trade-union leaders that it would lead to a general lowering of living standards** are unfounded if we consider the small number of people allowed in.

We are afforded, at little or no cost to ourselves, the opportunity of removing, once and for all, that background of suspicion which has prevented lasting friendship with our northern neighbours. It is a step well worth taking.

The WAP remained a bone of contention for many years. Australian attitudes towards Asians started to really soften in the early Sixties, and grew more sympathetic as that decade advanced. When the Whitlam Government came to power in the early Seventies, the complete change of stewardship saw the different attitudes of Australians actually put into action, and **started** the Asianisation of some suburbs in our big cities.

Another Asian issue in 1956 was **the recognition of Red China** by the UN and by other individual nations. Australia had not recognised China and, needless to say, nor had the

USA, though half the nations of the world **had** done so. Our problem was that we followed US foreign policy, and that demanded that we capitalist states should not recognise Communist China. So, over the last seven years, we had traded off and on with China, sometimes exchanged trade missions with each other, but still did everything we could to frustrate her moves into IndoChina and Malaya. We were even looking down our rifles at some Chinese in some regions right now. So we refused to recognise her, and also said "no" in the UN.

Still, the question of recognition would not go away.

William Deane, then a lecturer in International Law at Sydney University, wrote that any State, in considering whether to grant recognition to a new State, must first of all decide whether that new State will stand the test of time. If it decides the new nation will survive, then it must ask if it will abide by international law in all matters.

China appears to fail this second test, according to Deane. He cites its record of failing to respect the lives and property of foreign nationals, including missionaries, and their supposed military activity currently in Vietnam. He went on to conclude that China did not meet these requirements, and thus it should not be granted entry. Deane's words are of particular interest because, after a distinguished career, he went on to become Governor General of Australia.

I should point out for future clarity that the current Reds in China had been in power only since 1949. Then the previous Nationalist Government, led by Chiang Kai Shek, had been defeated after a civil war, and it had retreated to the island of Formosa. There, supported by America, it had set up a nuisance alternative Chinese Government, that subsequently harassed the mainland Chinese for many years until it stopped from boredom.

Letters, A H Sheehan. Your correspondent, William Deane has advanced the view that before recognition of a Government, it must (1) protect and respect the lives and property of foreign nationals; and (2) show that it is effective and stable.

If we were prepared to recognise Nazi Germany before 1939 – despite its atrocities – surely we must recognise the present Government of China.

Mr Selwn Speight's articles are convincing enough to show us that it is a Government supported by the people.

I suggest to William Deane that we act on events as they are, not as they should be, according to the law textbooks.

Letters, Louise MacInnes. It would be interesting to learn, on the basis of Mr W Deane's arguments against Australia's recognition of the Peoples' Republic of China, how he justifies the almost universal and immediate recognition of the present Guatemalan Government after it had seized power by a military putsch.

Violent revolutions in Argentina and sundry other South American Republics do not put them outside the international community.

Australia already recognises other Communist countries. Why should there be a special attitude to China?

Letters, A C Palfreeman. Until the international community achieves a much greater solidity than at present, and is in a position to enforce non-recognition as a serious sanction, it would seem to be in the interests of that community **to accept, nay, even to persuade,**

the black sheep to enter the fold, where at least it comes under the constant criticism and questioning around the conference table, and consequently in the world Press.

Too much reliance by the international community on the "good faith" referred to by Mr Deane may ultimately allow the black sheep to destroy the very conditions which tend to strengthen international law.

Comment. We did not recognise China until America did. This was after a surprise visit by President Nixon to China in the early 1970's. He returned saying that all was forgiven, and that we could all be good friends in the future. We rushed to join this entente cordiale.

MORE NEWS ON EGYPT

The Suez Canal is, of course, situated on Egypt's territory. Other nations are permitted to pass through the Canal under a Concession Agreement which is due to end in **1968 and then the Canal would revert to full Egyptian ownership.**

The Egyptian leader, Colonel Nasser, in front of a cheering crowd of 100,000, said that **Egyptian forces had seized the Canal**, and in future would run it. He will use the money to build the Aswan High Dam on the Nile. **"We will build the Dam on the skulls of 120,000 Egyptian workmen** who died in building the Suez Canal".

Maybe there is still a smidgen of animosity there somewhere.

JULY NEWS ITEMS

July 1st. Actress **Marilyn Monroe was married in New York**, at a secret wedding. Her husband was playwright Arthur Miller, and this was her third marriage. **After a low-key civil ceremony**, the wedding party went to the Miller family home, where **they feasted on chicken and potatoes**.

July 1st. In Sydney, when **the rise in tram fares came into effect**, a Scottish woman objected to the rise, and took a swipe at the conductress. **That lady said "I hit her back, and she threw the extra three pennies at me as she left the tram."** The rest of the trip, it was reported, was uneventful.

July 6th. **Today was a good day for Aussie sport in the UK.** Lew Hoad won the Wimbledon tennis. Peter Thompson won the British Open golf. This was his **third consecutive win**.

Five cadets from the Royal Military College at Duntroon were drowned when their two VJ dinghies capsized in a sudden wind while sailing on Lake George near Canberra.

Warning: **DANGER** ahead. The **prices of ice cream and ice blocks seem likely to rise** nationwide after price rises for ingredients in Melbourne. The increased costs of labour, and other materials, particularly sugar, are to blame.

The British Empire Cancer Campaign found no conclusive proof of a link between smoking and lung cancer. It injected tobacco tar into the lungs of **mice**, and found it made no difference. This was **very early days in the researching of links**, and the **now-conclusive** proof of a link came not from animals, but largely from **epidemiological studies** on **humans** that measured rates of impairment from smoking.

A Sydney woman is in a difficult position. **Her first husband** was reported missing from a Bass Strait steamer in 1949. **Later, the Courts had presumed her husband dead.** She **had remarried** and had a child by her second husband....

Now her first husband has reappeared. He had faked his fall from the steamer, and has been living in Melbourne "in a nightmare of dodging, evasion and fear of discovery." **He would very much like to resume his life with his former wife....**

She is refusing, and has begun proceedings for divorce. **The issue is clouded legally**, because he might be able to protest the divorce on the grounds of amnesia. The police are investigating the conduct of the man, and his disappearance.

July 25th. **Alice Springs was all agog** last night for the opening of the Australian movie *A Town Like Alice*. The main star, **Peter Finch,** was there and he had thrilled an air hostess on the trip up by inviting her to attend. She had done so. The author **Neville Shute** also attended....

The best quote from the night came from an old-timer, Bill Dibble, who had lived in Alice since 1910. He described the **town then as having "seven houses, three women, and no magic-lantern"**.

WHO WILL PAY FOR SCHOOLING?

For a long time, there had been much argument about proposals for the funding of non-State schools. Everyone was conscious of the fact that the Catholic schools, in particular, educated about a quarter of the nation's school children, and that they did this without any support from the various governments. As we will see, there was a long history to this non-funding situation, and also a long history of **mutual animosity between the various parties** as to whether any changes should be made.

At the moment, the Menzies Government, and some of the States, were making noises that suggested that some money should be given to the Catholic schools (and other private schools). For example, the Federal Government was about to make grants to encourage the building of scientific laboratories in all schools, including Catholic. There were other suggestions that run-down schools, often in church buildings, should be given building grants to upgrade.

The point of objection for some people was that this was seen as the thin edge of the wedge. Once the process of granting money to Catholic schools was started, surely it would grow and grow until the Catholics were on an equal footing with the State-run secular schools.

The arguments, though, ranged wider than that. Here are just **two arguments that the Catholics put forward**. **One** was that the State schools scarcely mentioned God, yet this God, and all matters connected with him, were of paramount importance to all children. Why should this Christian state continue to deny religious education, and thus provide an inadequate education, and at the same time, tax Catholics for the money to provide such education?

Two, completely different, was that suppose every Catholic child in schooling turned up one day at the local public school. There was no doubt that the system could not cope, and that it would descend into immediate chaos.

Then **there were arguments for the secularists**. **One** sample **argument** was that the Catholics were offered a free education, along with the majority. If they wanted to do their own thing, then that was well and good, but why should the already-burdened tax-payer have to pay for the idiosyncrasies of a minority?

A **second** argument was that **the State and churches were now separate from each other**, and that this was now a well-established practice in all civilised countries. Clearly, if the State started to subsidise church schools, this separation no longer existed, and the "terrible days prior to the French Revolution would be upon us again".

So, arguments erupted throughout society. The *SMH* was not spared, and its Letters columns were dominated by the issue for three full weeks. Many of the matters raised were variants of the ones I included above, but there were others of equal interest that I think worthy of reporting.

Letters, J O'Shea. Methodist and other Protestant spokesmen do not impress unbiased citizens with their protests **against financial aid to denominational schools**, for it is obvious that they themselves will benefit little from such aid, owing to **the insignificant number of children educated at Methodist schools**.

Indeed, it is by adopting such un-Christian attitudes of "what I don't want you cannot have" type that causes religious bitterness in the community. Before such minority groups air their displeasure, it would be wise of them to consider the actual numerical denominational position existing in private schools today, which is: Church of England, 7 percent; Catholic, 89 per cent; Presbyterian, 2 per cent; Methodist, 1 per cent.

Letters, D B Knox, Moore Theological College, Newtown. The charge of your correspondent J O'Shea against Protestant church leaders that they are acting in an unchristian way when they object to State aid to Roman Catholic schools, having few schools of their own, ignores a very pertinent fact of history.

Up till 1880 the educational policy of the Government of New South Wales was a dual school system, and it granted financial aid to both State schools and church and private schools.

In that year, the Government adopted a policy of a single school system, and asked the Churches to cooperate by closing their own schools and teaching religion in the State schools. The Protestant Churches, even when preferring the former system, agreed to the Government's request. They allowed their numerous church schools to close, and taught without pay in the State schools. The Roman Catholic Church refused to do either.

Comment. The Letter from Rev Knox was not only informative and interesting, it also sparked a discussion as to whether historical facts from 60 years ago were still pertinent today. So many things have changed that surely the ideas from long ago were no longer relevant. Yet, history does explain somewhat why some Protestant churches were not providing their own education. Surely, it was, at long last, right for the failures of the past to be rectified. The debate continued. But we will return to the "state aid for schools" issue.

Letters, (Rev) T P McEvoy, Presbyterian Church of Australia. Already in tax rebates for school fees, the Federal Government has yielded to pressure, and **any fresh encroachment** which will further the principle of aid for Church schools **is being watched anxiously** by those who hold the view that the organisers of the separate denominational school should be prepared to meet the outlay involved and not to saddle the community with more than one educational system. This is the attitude adopted throughout the Commonwealth by the Presbyterian Church.

The constitutional position as to whether the Churches receiving such aid would thereby become "established" Churches is one that might readily deter the Government from proceeding with the proposed financial aid.

Australia is still young, and in the formative stage, **cannot afford the luxury of maintaining two systems of education**, the one affirming the principle of national solidarity and offering equal facilities to every child; the other, the Church school, in effect segregational and, therefore, tending to retard the building up within this nation of one undivided people.

Letters, Live and Let Live. It seems to me that the opposition of State aid to private schools is prompted by jealousy.

The plain fact is that Protestant pastors, knowing they are in the majority in the private schools' effort, are willing to forgo any financial aid, so as to hit at their Catholic fellow-Christians, who are making a prodigious effort in the educational field, and making a big saving to the State. What sort of Christianity is it that ignores the most important of virtues, that of charity? Is it any wonder that so many churches are empty and bankrupt spiritually?

Letters, R M Gascoigne. Education, to be effective, must centre about the whole child; to do this it must know what the child is. Few people will deny (and none can rationally deny) that man is a composite being of spirit and matter, and that **his destiny is God.** Is it not unreal to pretend to be educating a child whilst deliberately leaving out the essential thing?

Secular education is a contradiction in terms. It will not do to say that the home must make up the deficiency. The home does not and cannot; even if it had the will it could not put back into the child's education the centre, the point of reference, which has been left out.

Comment. At this stage, the Editor of the *SMH* stopped the correspondence. As is often the case, when so many people are involved, and so many unthinking prejudices are displayed, the arguments were set to go on and on.

Of course, it still goes on today, even though the various governments provide liberal funding to non-State schools. But today, the proportion of religious schools has increased rapidly, and their prestige generally has gained so much, that no government would dare to turn back the clock.

DISCRIMINATION AGAINST SOME

The Federal Government's small-arms factory at the NSW country town of Lithgow had just about come to the end of its war-time usefulness, and was being gradually closed down. This meant that a few hundred workers were to be dismissed. The appropriate authorities announced that the first to go should be women, followed by New Australians, and then single men.

This raised howls of protest from the community. Protestors claimed that this was discriminatory, and that some other basis for the reduction should be found. But, the argument was not about the high place of women on the list – as it would be today – but about the unhappy decision to **sack New Australians second**. I will address this latter point first, **then come back to the plight of the women**.

The million New Australians in the nation were clearly up in arms. Letters poured in.

Letters, Mavis A Wybenga. I was amazed and, as an Australian, ashamed to read the statement attributed to Sir Eric Harrison that dismissals from the Lithgow Small Arms Factory should be in the order of women first, followed by New Australians, and then single Australian men.

New Australians, apparently, are invited to this country because Australia has an urgent need of them. They may be allowed to work when there are too few workers for the jobs available, but when any industrial or economic reverse occurs, they are to be tossed aside like a squeezed lemon.

As the wife of one of these "second-class" citizens, who must register for National Service as soon as they become of eligible age, but may not be naturalised for five years; who in the State may **build** Housing Commission homes, but may not **occupy** one; and now, may earn their living in times of plentiful work, but not otherwise, let me register my protest.

Sir Eric's "explanation" that 90 per cent of the New Australians to be dismissed are late-comers is irrelevant to the principle involved. If the dismissals are necessary and the Government wishes to use the "last to come, first to go" principle, the term "New Australian" should not at any stage become involved.

Letters, One of the Second-Class. May I express my sincerest thanks to Sir Eric Harrison for telling me, a New Australian, and an ex-member of her Majesty's forces, clearly where I stand in this country.

Are these the views of his whole Government? In that case, will his words and actions be followed by some of his colleagues as, for example, the Treasury taking taxes first from old Australians, and only later from second-class New Australians? For surely, if we do not deserve the same consideration in employment, we should also be treated differently in other respects.

The 1,300,000 second-class New Australians, and a few more hundreds of thousands of prospective immigrants still overseas, are gratified to be told for once, frankly, where their place is.

Letters, Oscar A Guth. Your second leader on June 7 asks, "When does a New Australian cease to be New Australian?" and goes on to say that "there is a very strong case for dropping the classification" on naturalisation of the person.

The question is fully answered in Australia's certificate of Naturalisation, which says that the naturalised person named in the document shall "have to all intents and purposes the status of an Australian citizen and British subject."

Nowhere in this or any other connected document is it stated that the person has been, is or shall ever be, referred to by anyone as a New Australian – and perhaps least of all by a Minister of the Crown.

The term is a pure invention which has no official status whatsoever, and is felt to be offensive by the majority of migrants who know the United States has carried out a vastly greater and more successful immigration programme without ever using any such discriminatory term, such as "New American" for instance.

Note however that our society held quite a few people who were opposed to our support for massive migration into the country from Europe. Most of these complained that they were taking up our jobs and our housing. Some simply disliked the "wogs" and "dagoes" and for them, that was argument enough.

When it came to **dismissal notices for women,** there were few complaints. In fact, a woman, writing to argue that New Australians had equal rights with locals, ended with "would it not have been better for Sir Eric to announce that the order of dismissal **should have been women first** followed by single men?"

One lonely voice pleaded the case for women, and that was a bit half-hearted.

Letters, Rearguard. No doubt all Australians – old and new – will be relieved at the policy of our Liberal Government, as expressed by Sir Eric Harrison, who has assured us that it will only be the women, after all, who will be "humping the bluey" should depression come.

Such a chivalrous, gentlemanly attitude! But women, of course, particularly single ones, are too few to form pressure groups and since their men have, in the main, been killed off in two wars, who will worry about them?

Comment. Sir Eric Harrison repented, and announced that the principle of "last on, first off" would apply. This seemed like a reasonable way to proceed, and raised the question of why it was not used from the beginning.

In any case, you can see that today's feminism was a long way off in 1956. Voices would have been much louder today. The fact was that the **man was still generally regarded as the bread winner**, and that his income was to be used to support a family of six. The idea that family status should be ignored in allocating jobs was not widely accepted by men, nor widely argued by women.

NEWS FROM THE BACK-BLOCKS

Outback Australia, back in 1956, rarely made the news in the cities. Information from the 99 per cent of Australia that extended outside of the cities was quite limited. Stories that **were** always published talked about floods and droughts, the price of wheat, strikes by shearers, the bad state of the roads, locust plagues and dust storms. I have selected below a few **other** Letters that will give you an idea of what our country cousins were talking about.

The roo shooting season. Regulations for the shooting of wildlife varied across the nation. **Most of the nation had no such regulations**, and in most semi-occupied regions, **any regulations were ignored**. It was part of the outback tradition that lone hunters and organised hunting parties would venture into the vast outback spaces and shoot at will.

Some Councils and States at times thought that this slaughter was going too far, and posted regulations that said it should stop, or that it should be restricted to certain "seasons". Thus we had duck-shooting seasons, and similar seasons for roos, rabbits, emus and the like.

There were many arguments as to the whole question of the culling of animals. This Letter touches on the broader subject.

Letters, R F Hundy. Apparent misrepresentation regarding the marsupial population in the Mudgee district has been responsible for yet another open season being declared against kangaroos, wallaroos and wallabies for a period of two months from May 18.

Surely the Chief Secretary is not so naïve or out of touch with country conditions not to know that an open season is in operation 12 months of the year (unofficially of course).

This has been a very important contributing factor **in the rapidly declining number of marsupials in this area**.

The unvarnished facts are:

(1)   Marsupials are hunted all the year round by individual shooters and unofficial hunting parties.

(2) Properties in the area are comparatively small, and property dog-packs take heavy toll of those animals rash enough to wander in from rough and unimproved parts.

(3) Since the near-annihilation of the rabbit, kangaroos, wallaroos, etc. are eagerly sought after as dog feed.

What, then, does the declaration of an open season achieve? It not only gives added impetus to the activities of local hunters, but encourages organised shooters from outside centres to invade the district.

It allows those who have collected marsupial skins in the 'unofficial' season to dispose of them, and at greatly enhanced values.

By giving official sanction to the needless slaughter, the younger generation is encouraged to develop a ghoulish disregard towards the preservation of Australian fauna.

I emphasise that marsupials in this district are not so numerous as to warrant an official season for indiscriminate and widespread slaughter.

Wait for a farm. At the start of WWI and WWII, the Army was anxious to recruit volunteers to put on the uniform and go off and kill Huns. One inducement they offered was that, on return, they would be given parcels of land in the country, and also assistance to set up as farmers or graziers. After WW1, Soldiers Settlements were established in some areas, and generally they failed because of lack of farming experience, inadequate capital, and the vagaries of the weather. After WWII, land was again being allocated by the Government, but as the following Letter tells, the road to riches on this highway was meeting many blockages.

Letters, Mrs G E Wright. As one vitally interested in soldier settlement, I would like to ask, is there no way in which the Government can expedite settlement?

My husband, who served six years in the AIF during World War II, first began applying for **ballots** in June, 1944, whilst he was serving in New Guinea. After 12 years of applying for hundreds of ballots, **he is no nearer now to being settled than when he first began applying**.

The promotion scheme, where an eligible ex-Serviceman who is the holder of a Qualification Certificate, may, if he is able to locate an owner willing to offer his property, lodge an application to acquire the farm, seems unsatisfactory. My husband has never yet been able to find an owner prepared to sell a block through this scheme. Most vendors say they would be prepared to sell, but that it takes too long for the Government to reach a decision as to whether the property and the price are acceptable.

Why not a series of **hard-luck ballots** for the hundreds of men who have been applying unsuccessfully for more than seven or eight years?

NEWS AND VIEWS

Letters, J Huddleston. You rightly criticise the spoilers of the bushland. However, my council collects only once a year and will only pick up certain rubbish. It was far-sighted enough to say that rubbish accumulated between collections may be taken to its tip, but it has since put up a fence and a gate which is closed at week ends. Apparently people can only take their rubbish there in their working time.

An adjacent council has a notice on its tip that anyone depositing rubbish there will be prosecuted. I think that councils are basically the cause of the people taking their rubbish to beauty spots.

NEWS FROM NULLA NULLA

The NSW town of **Coonabarabran is cranky**. A movie, to be made by a Hollywood syndicate, and set in the township, is being made with a lot of movieland publicity and gusto. The movie is *The Shiralee,* and Peter Finch will be the star. This is great for the local economy, and **the locals were very excited**. **The problem** is that in the movie, the township will be named as **Nulla Nulla.** This is supposedly for (unspecified) legal reasons. Inter alia, the film-makers are on the lookout for **a local girl who can play a vamp** in a scene with Finch.

AN UPDATE ON EGGS

In future, eggs will be sold only in cartons. These will be sealed and carry a date so that old eggs cannot be sold.

AUGUST NEWS ITEMS

August 1ˢᵗ. The NSW Government will allow licensed clubs to legally operate poker machines. The churches are against this increase in the opportunity to gamble, and the clubs – **secretly delighted** – are moaning about the increased level of fees they will have to pay....

These fees will be **ear-marked for the support of hospitals** (what a joke), and will be charged on machines that accept coins ranging from sixpence to two shillings. **About 1,000 clubs in NSW will be eligible to use the machines**, and they are mainly RSLs, Workers', and sporting clubs.

August 1ˢᵗ. As an avid Australian cricket-lover, I advise you that **the following paragraph is not worth reading, and you should skip over it**. The information in it is aberrant, and abhorrent....

England won the Ashes at Old Trafford, in Manchester, after **Jim Laker bowled out the entire Australian side for 53 runs**. That is right.... he took all 10 wickets for 53. **It brought his total for the match to 19 for 93.** Clearly he was very devious, and there should be some way of bringing a protest. **You should just forget I mentioned the game at all**.

A truckload of branded and sacked potatoes has been stolen in Melbourne. It is believed that the thieves will try to sell them in Sydney because of the high prices there. Police along the main traffic routes to Sydney have been alerted, and **any truck carrying potatoes will be searched** for a particular brand on the sacks.

A Royal Guardsman was strolling yesterday in St James Park near Buckingham Palace. He was dressed in the off-duty "uniform" of the guards, with a stiff white collar, dark blue suit, bowler hat and umbrella....

Prince Charles, Princess Anne and a nurse hove to with one of the Queen's corgis. It got excited, started yapping loudly, and **tore the seat out of the guardsman's trousers.** Prince Charles was most apologetic. Another corgi was in trouble two years ago when it **bit a Royal sentry on the ankle.**

A New Australian plans to bag 100 7-foot crocodiles. He will stuff and mount them, and plans to **sell them as souvenirs to American tourists at the Olympics.**

The Treasurer, Sir Arthur Fadden, brought down the **annual Oz Budget** at the end of the month. This year he decided that **the slug would be to postal rates**, and the normal increases on tobacco and grog would not happen. All in all, the Budget suggested that **the nation was doing rather well....**

Sir Arthur also announced that **our migrant annual intake would be reduced to 115,000 from 133,000....**

This was because of the constant clamour from some sources that migrants were taking the jobs away from locals, and that they took a lot of resources, with little immediate payback.

AN INDUSTRIAL DISPUTE

I remind you again that strikes by workers were occurring without warning every day. Most of these did not concern serious issues, but were capricious, or were part of a vendetta, or were simply bloody-minded. In many cases, the management and the workers were equally at fault, and a bit of goodwill and commonsense would have worked wonders. Take this report below as an example.

Mail sorters at the Sydney GPO are now on a work-to-regulations strike. That means they will still sort many envelopes, but will reject any that carry advertising, have too little detail in the address, or too much detail in the address (such as Granville **and** Sydney), and which have window-type cellulose fronts that supposedly reflect light and affect sorters' eyes.

This means that Sydney **business-houses** will receive back 200,000 pieces of mail that they posted last week. They will have to be **returned by hand** because, since they do not comply with regulations, they cannot be returned by mail. At the same time, breaches of other regulations have held up delivery of 250,000 **private letters** to households.

Obviously, this strike had nothing to do with the regulations. In fact, it sprang from the fact that a fair bit of mail was being pilfered by the sorters, so that management locked a dozen doors to stop them from leaving the building during work hours. The workers, horrified by any suggestions that any sorter would ever steal mail, decided to work to regulations in protest.

Management, after a few days, relented and said that they would unlock the doors. And they did that, except for five doors. The workers were not happy with this, and added another day to the strike. Meanwhile, last week's letters were still being returned by hand. At the end, the five doors were unlocked, and the sorting, and presumably the pilfering, continued as before.

Comment. There is not much I can add. The folly of this is obvious, as is the abiding division between management and Labor.

THE SUEZ CANAL

Half the countries of the world were today talking about getting rid of the former colonial powers that had occupied their lands and exploited their resources for centuries. The Brits, French and Dutch were conspicuous here, and they were now at various stages of leaving their former colonies to their own devices. In **some** cases, power had already passed smoothly to the local population, while in **other nations**, the transmission had been, and still was, marked with violence and often armed rebellion.

For the Brits, the suddenness of Nasser's decision was all the more shocking because it was portrayed as the **nationalisation** of the Canal. This was unfortunate because for ten years the world had seen industry after industry in Britain "socialised" by the post-war Labor Government, and no one was at all convinced that this had improved anything. Now, to have their much-lauded canal "nationalised" by their former servants was both unpleasant and alarming. Where would it end?

So the British Government erupted into a frenzy of activity. Military Reserves were called up, troops were sent to

Cyprus and other places near to Egypt, ambassadors were recalled, angry speeches and threats were made. Egyptian assets were frozen world-wide, existing staff working in the Canal Zone were evacuated, and British troops were even kitted out in tropical clothing.

After a couple of weeks of posturing, it was decided that 22 interested nations would meet in London, and there they would discuss – and hopefully approve – a proposal that would say that control of the Canal would pass to an international body, and that Egypt would be allowed to join that august body.

Colonel Nasser was not at all interested in this. He had settled on his approach, and **was adamant that Egypt, and Egypt alone, would have control over the Canal, and that it alone would collect all revenue from there**. Egypt did not attend the 22-nation conference, but all the while, Nasser remained quite steady and determined, as the other chooks clucked and preened.

By the end of the month, a second conference was proposed. This time, a 5-power Committee was to be sent to Egypt, and this, believe it or not, **was to be led by none other than our own Bob Menzies**. This worthy gentleman had been in New York and London when Nasser nationalised the Canal, and since then he had been in the forefront of all discussions on the subject, hobnobbing with the mightiest men in Britain and the world. **Now**, we were told that **he,** delaying his return to Oz **another** month, would lead this deputation to the Land of the Pharaohs, and probably and hopefully, it would be **he** who would arrive back in Britain with an umbrella and a scrap of paper just like Chamberlain did almost 20 years earlier.

This, at the end of August, was the mighty vision that the Press conjured up in Oz, much of it with a chest swollen with pride. Just how it will work out, I will leave until events unfold next month.

LETTERS ON EGYPT AND THE SUEZ

As you might imagine, these events developed in a short time and created a lot of noise in the Editorial and Letters columns. I have picked out a few comments that illustrate some aspects of what was a very complex situation.

Letters, S T Kelly. While most people appreciate the seriousness of the Suez Canal position, only the extreme partisan would deny the right of Colonel Nasser and the Egyptian Government to terminate an agreement which affects wholly Egyptian territory and which would terminate within a few years anyway.

Those who attack one-nation control would have a case, perhaps, if the free passage of ships through the canal was hindered. This has not yet happened – unless, perhaps, in the case of Israel – but no voices have been raised in protest.

The safest and only democratic procedure is for the Western Powers to press, through the United Nations, for the international control of **all** canals joining seas or oceans. The profit from the canals could go to UN funds and this would remove the real bone of contention – the canal profits.

Comment. This moderate Letter stayed well away from the initial hysterical British position that Nasser should be routed by military force. Mr Kelly suggests UN control would be the answer. But, along with many others, he does not realise that Nasser is in control of the land and assets of the Canal, and like all other nations, **he wants the control and the profits from exploiting his own nation's land**. The benefits should go to Egypt, he says, not to anyone else, including the UN.

Letters, R J Keegan. Any interruption of the normal flow of oil to Britain and Australia – and the normal flow would be very seriously interrupted if tankers had to go round the Cape – would paralyse activity in both countries, bring industry to a halt, and cause wholesale unemployment. Such is our dependence on oil today. It can also be taken for granted that any threat to its Middle East oil supplies would force the United States to prohibit the export of oil from any American source.

While ordinary trade through the canal is also threatened, there is little doubt, I think, that is the threat to their oil supplies that is causing so much concern in the United Kingdom and France, and forcing them to take military precautions for its protection. Even a rudimentary knowledge of the area with its oilfields and its maze of pipelines is sufficiently convincing of what can be done as a result of whipped-up nationalism, and the resulting nationalisation and harm to the Western world.

It is sheer mischievous nonsense to bring colonialism, imperialism, or any other 'ism' (except communism) into this sorry business, and the time has surely come for the United Nations to assume control and responsibility for this and any other international waterway.

Comment. The above Letter is another voice advocating that the UN gets control, but again ignoring Egypt's sovereign right.

Letters, Max Freilich, President, Zionist Federation of Australia. We have read with keen interest your editorials on Egypt's nationalisation of the Suez Canal, and wish to congratulate you on having been clear in emphasising the fact that Egypt's denial of the Suez Canal to Israel was symptomatic of Egypt's general unreliability and presumption in the matter of international obligations.

It is the writer's hope that Australia, and every other maritime nation deeply concerned in the absolute freedom of the canal for all peoples without a single exception, will champion no settlement that does not fully and uncompromisingly restore that **freedom of the canal** under international control **to Israel also**.

Merely to return to the present situation, in which Israel traffic can be blocked at will by Egypt, would be to leave entirely unsolved the real crux of the present problem between the Western Powers and Egypt. Nothing else than a settlement unmistakably including Israel in the enjoyment of unhindered freedom of the canal can be acceptable to Australia.

Comment. Since the takeover, Nasser had run the business-side of the Canal without a hitch to anyone. Except for his old arch-enemy, Israel. He had refused permission for ships from that nation to pass through the Canal. This in fact was a side-issue, but it did send out a warning: if other nations fell foul of Egypt, might this international waterway be closed to them also?

Letters, R W Robson. The contemptible little squeaks emerging from the Federal Labor Party on the subject of the Suez crisis and Mr Menzies's activities in London give the measure of the Labor Party's contribution to any discussion of world affairs.

I am no admirer of the Commonwealth Government which Mr Menzies, for his sins, is fated to lead; but, since the retirement of Churchill, I (and, I think, most well-informed people) regard Mr Menzies as the outstanding statesman of the British Commonwealth.

It was sheer luck that he was in the United States when the Suez crisis "broke," and was able to present the British viewpoint, clearly and unequivocally, to Washington. It was greater luck that he was able to return to London to support Britain in her no-further-retreat stand, in opposition to the anti-colonialists, led by Dulles, and the neutralists, led by Nehru.

Apparently, most of our politicians and commentators cannot realise that Suez actually is the culminating point in a process that has been going on since World War II; and that, if we do not stand firm now – with all the risks that may involve – we shall see **the collapse of the British Commonwealth within a decade.** Surrendering now to Egypt (and to the idle fellow-travellers directed by Moscow) may save our skins and our bank balances **in 1956**; but it would make our **enslavement by Muscovite communism** certain **by 1966**. That is why we are happy to see Mr Menzies sitting in at this vital conference in support of Eden and Selwyn Lloyd. May he stay there to the end.

Comment. Ra! Ra! Go, Ming.

Finally here, a Mr Bentley, from Fairy Meadow, wrote a long Letter in which he pointed out that Australia had entered into innumerable contracts with foreign countries to allow them to use **our** national facilities. He considered that Australia could close those contracts, pay compensation, and then be on exactly the same footing as the Egyptian Government was in nationalising the Canal.

Comment. You won't be surprised to learn that there will be more Letters next month.

RELIABILITY TRIALS

The Redex Trials were first held in 1953. Starting from Sydney, the 200 cars involved drove northwards up to about Cairns, then westwards into the Northern Territory, thence to Adelaide and Melbourne, and back to Sydney. The whole trip took in 6,500 miles, and hit the headlines for about two weeks.

The idea of these Trials was to provide makers and buyers with information about the reliability of ordinary household cars. It might help the manufacturers design new vehicles, and at the same time help buyers make decisions on their next purchase. The first three annual Trials were sponsored by Redex, and the 1956 event by Ampol.

The first Trial got the whole nation excited. Crowds of people met contestants at every conceivable point, the Press coverage was everywhere, and closing and greeting ceremonies met the fleet at strategic points. Over the next couple of years, some of the early enthusiasm wore off, as people counted the cost.

A few people were killed as the cars drove the track at break-neck speed, hundreds were injured, roads and property of all sorts were destroyed, and menageries of roos, wombats and other animals were slaughtered. As well as that, the drivers and the teams supporting the cars were extremely keen to do well, and used almost any means, sometimes fair and sometimes a bit foul, to get a high placing. No one actually said that anyone was cheating, so I will simply say that they were all truly very competitive.

So, society was rethinking the future of the Trials, and asking what changes could be made to eliminate the problems.

Letters, Gwydir Henry. When I watched the arrival in Grafton on Saturday last of contestants in the Ampol trial, I was filled with admiration for the two young men in the MG car. Here was a small, open car, pitted against luxurious closed cars of up to four times the power, yet they were running in third place in the trial. The whole community was shocked **to learn a few hours later of the tragic end of these two intrepid men.**

What is the sense in these trials? The time has long since passed for trials to prove the reliability of present-day cars. All present-day cars are reliable. They are built of world-proved components, by firms with years of experience, and it rests with owners whether they get good service from their cars or not.

Proof of reliability can easily be observed by a drive on any highway. Years ago, when cars were few, it was a common sight to see cars stranded on the roads, but today, when cars have increased a hundredfold, it is a rare thing to see a car broken down.

Letters, R Ellison. Mr Gwydir Henry asks "What is the sense of the present car trials?"

This question, just as logically applied to cricket, football, boxing, surfing, skiing and so on, can elicit no answer save the pleasure of individual participation in a sport for sport's sake.

That this answer, in a nation with Australia's traditional love of sport, is sufficient, is surely borne out by the fact that, year after year, many of the same competitors take the field.

Yet Mr Henry's own letter has provided a justification for these very reliability trials. "It is a rare thing to see a car broken down" today – only because manufacturers of modern cars, in studying automotive efficiency, have confirmed their own finding by the results of such trials.

PORTERS NOT AT WORK

Most readers will remember the class of railway worker called porters. These gentlemen and lads used to present for work daily, and the job included the carrying of goods and luggage from one place to another. Most country towns, apart from a very important Station Master, had a porter as well, and these workers managed the affairs of about thirty passengers and six trains a day. In the cities, the porters could be recognised by their distinctive crumpled and incomplete uniforms, and the packs that they loitered in, sullenly, between their meal breaks.

Letters, (Rev) N Ward. There is one section of the New South Wales Government railways which should come in for its share of criticism, namely, the people who do the portering. My experience last Friday morning has left me with a feeling that there is something wrong in that department.

I took my wife and small girl in to catch a train to Junee. We were running a bit late and, after unloading my passengers with their luggage, I said to go for the train and I would try to get back in time to see them off after finding a parking place.

I got back to the platform in time to see the train pulling out and my wife in some distress looking for me. She had asked a porter to help her with her small amount of luggage to get to Platform 15, and the answer was, "Me 'eart's too bad." They missed the train and two booked seats.

I would suggest either a medical examination of the staff, or a determination by some responsible person as to whether porters should be allowed to do the job of portering.

Comment. The Reverend sadly had the wrong ideas about porters. He thought that they were employed to help passengers, and perhaps he thought that they might spring to the task, with or without a tip.

My observation, and that of hundreds of oldies I have spoken to, is that this was not the case. I did hear about one nice young man who helped a women with five children in Condobolin, but that was **his first day at work**, before he had learned the ropes. Then there was a second porter at Walgett who assisted an old lady with one leg and a parrot on her shoulder, but she was his grandmother and Irish.

DON'T DESPAIR

Letters, Joseph Bernard. My son and I were on a railway tourist excursion to the Jenolan Caves on August 19, and among the party were four lady schoolteachers and 24 girl pupils, from Fairfield Public school, their ages ranging from about 8 to 10 years. The attention given those children by the teachers was more than even a mother could give them, and I admired those teachers for being such angels as to give up their weekend for the enjoyment of the children. And did those children enjoy themselves!

If those young women represent the spirit of this modern age, God bless them all!

Comment. Porters do not set the pace for the country. Hope still exists, as shown by these teachers and girls.

LIFE AT UNIVERSITY IN 1956

Life was bliss for uni students, though they might not have realised it at the time. Most of them were there on Bob Menzies' Commonwealth Scholarships that paid their fees. They also gave students a living allowance, and this meant they could keep skin and bone together without getting a part-time job. So they could spend the whole week on campus, as full-time students should. Some of them thus got a good education, rather then just a bunch of tickets.

When they left Uni, they had no HECS debt. The idea of user-pays for education was a later development.

Like I said, it was a great time to go to university. As I look at kids now, I feel sorry that they miss out on a grand experience.

LUXURIES FOR CLERGY

The **Church of England** Synod in Sydney decided yesterday that **washing machines and refrigerators should not be provided in clergymen's rectories**....

Opinions. "I do not think that to provide these sets an example of **Christian self-sacrifice**. How can we ask people who do not have them to provide them for a rectory?" "It is bordering on **sheer lunacy** to provide these things." "It will not help clergy in **their personal contacts** to have them." The Synod, in its wisdom, agreed that such benefits were too lavish, and would promote envy.

SEPTEMBER NEWS ITEMS

The Federal Government is **now regularly importing Rhesus monkeys so that the Salk anti-polio vaccine** can be made from their bodies. Recently, a baby monkey was born on the air-trip to Australia. It was decided that **this baby, and its mother, should be spared the death penalty**, and would instead be housed at Melbourne zoo. Sir Edward Hallstrom would meet any costs. The Feds replied that there would be no such costs in this case.

In the **largest cattle-duffing raids in Queensland history, 800 bulls have been stolen** from a property in the central-west of the State. The theft was discovered when the bulls were being mustered for sale. They are all carrying Queensland brands, but police say that these can be altered easily.

September 13ᵗʰ. Postal workers in Sydney are on strike again. This time for a two Pound a week wage rise. Once again, they are sorting mail according to their version of "regulations". A **million and a half articles are waiting to be sorted**, and many of them had been returned to sender. **Two days later,** two million letters were held up **and 125,000 parcels....**

The work-to-regulation strike is a good weapon because workers can still say they turned up, and did a fair day's work. **That means they still get paid.**

The US film *Rock Around the Clock* had **its first showing** in Australia tonight at the Victory Theatre in Sydney. The audience was made up of **gaudily-dressed bodgies and widgies**, who were stamping their feet, were singing and whistling, and abusive. Still, **they did not riot as they had in the US and Britain.**

September 17th. **Postal workers** at a mass meeting accepted the union executive decision to **return to normal work.** Three men who had been suspended during the strike were reinstated, and **the workers did not get their pay rise.**

It had to happen. The retailers of news services, film providers, and TV channels **right round the world had pooled together** months ago to **negotiate deals** with the Australian Government and the Olympic Committee. It was claimed that the pool represented 500,000,000 customers who wanted to get news or vision of **the Olympics in Melbourne** in November....

In later September, it was announced that **negotiations had broken down over a number of matters.** For example, the Committee was reported to want payment of a sum of money for the right to report on the Olympics. The media, however, said **all Olympic events were news stories**, and so no fee should be payable, and that **they would not cover the Olympic Games at all.** This clearly was a negotiating ploy, and given that there was six weeks to go, there was no need for panic by anyone....

It was the beginning of the new era where copyright on **events** had to be paid for, and the start of the **huge money payments** that are now paid for **all sporting events.**

THE SUEZ CRISIS

The big news event of the month of September was the Suez Crisis. You will remember that on July 26th, President Nasser nationalised the Canal, and said that in future all moneys, and all control, would be for the benefit of Egypt. He said that it would still remain an international waterway, and that all ships would be allowed to pass. But that he was determined that its full ownership would be vested in Egypt.

That was the position at the start of September. And that was exactly the same position at the end.

Of course, Britain and France were most upset by this. They had the most to lose, because they had funded the Canal in the first place, and remained the major shareholders in the Company running it up to the takeover. So throughout this month, they bluffed and blustered as only frustrated former colonial powers can do.

They sent off Menzies to persuade Nasser. He did no good at all, and returned talking tough about sanctions and using force. They had meetings of 26 nations, that dwindled to 18 nations, and then fell to 14 nations. These were hopeful that some sort of international body would assume authority over the Canal and, jolly good of them, Egypt would be part of this.

In the meantime, the Brits and French were playing chicken with the idea of military force. They were sending military equipment and manpower to the Middle East at a rapid rate. So much so, for example, that Australian shippers were complaining that they could get no boats to carry their goods overseas.

The wilder British newspapers were urging Britain to **storm the Canal**, and were running stories about supposed threats by the Egyptians to scuttle ships in it, and so block it to all users.

All the while, the Egyptians were arresting or deporting Brits as spies, and the Brits were doing what they could to ensure other nations would **close off all supplies of money and credit to the Egyptians**. The hope was that Nasser would be forced to the negotiating table by scarcity of money, but this strategy was scuppered when the US-based IMF granted the Egyptians a big loan for the duration.

So, with all this going on, it became obvious that Nasser would not budge. The 14 nations had talked themselves hoarse, and many were throwing up their hands in resignation. After all, why not just accept it, some said. The traffic is still flowing through the Canal, the costs and services are the same. The only difference was that profits were now going to the home country, rather than to foreigners. This latter idea appealed to dozens of third-world nations who were struggling for their own independence from colonial powers.

So, by the end of September, the Brits and France and others, **decided to refer the matter to the UN**. There were many who argued that here was where the dispute should have been all along. **In any case, grave matters of Empire were in the balance.** Could **a once-colonial nation simply nationalise** enterprises and promise compensation, and thereafter run them themselves for their own benefit?

We will wait with anxiety for next month's installment.

MENZIES' ROLE

Menzies came in for his fair share of criticism, but it was along Party lines. He had gone off to Egypt, heralded by the world Press as the chosen one to lead the British back into Egypt. But he had come back again, with only conventional words of wisdom to back him. He had had his moment, a week in which he basked in the attendance of the leaders of the Free World, and now it was gone.

The Labor Party enjoyed this a lot. It had not been pleasant to see their foe strutting the stage in London, and now he was a mere mortal again. The Liberals remembered the hours of glory, and welcomed him as a great statesman. But....

Letter, H C Beere, Dorset, England. May a quite unimportant Englishman, who cherishes a deep affection for Australia and her warm-hearted people, beg a little space in your columns to pay tribute to the character and ability of your great Prime Minister?

The dignity and restraint with which he has performed a difficult and, indeed, almost impossible task, deserve the highest praise. He has become a world statesman of whom you may all be rightly proud.

Letter, W F Wilson. The speech on the Suez Canal by Menzies was a most regrettable effort. It was ill-timed, as Dr Evatt so wisely pointed out, and was not the sort of utterance that responsible leaders like Eisenhower or Dulles would have made.

Australia, and the cause of world peace, would have been better served if the Minister for External Affairs, Casey, had been allowed to handle the delicate situation as the Australian representative. As it was, we had the usual performance that is to expected of Menzies. Firstly, bully and bluster, and a straining for rhetorical effect. Secondly, really little more than superficial acquaintance with the underlying motives of the issues to which he addressed himself.

The Press is doing a grave disservice to Australia and its status in responsible world leadership by giving such sycophantic support to Menzies. Dr Evatt was the realist of Tuesday's debate, and I am sure, that in his heart, Casey agreed with the reasoned and truly moving exposition that the Labor leader made of the situation.

WHAT'S THAT DOING ON THE WALL?

Each year, the Council of the Sydney suburb of Mosman conducts an art festival. In 1954, and thereafter, it banned **modern art** entries on the grounds that they were unintelligible to the man in the street. Early in this month, however, they changed their collective mind and granted the First Prize to **an abstract** painting called Obelisque. The winner, Max Feuerring, won a prize of 80 Guineas.

The decision was not easily reached. One Councillor said "the winning entry is beyond my understanding. I sat in front of it for half an hour, and all I could do was imagine it as an advertisement by a corset manufacturer saying: Girls, do not let this happen to you".

Another said "Frankly, this winning entry horrified me. A Council is a place where dignified paintings should be hung, and frankly this is far from being one." **There were others who thought differently.** "If you took a poll of aldermen round the State, you would find that most of them want paintings of their predecessors grouped around their mayor. We in Mosman should not revert to such **a low attitude of mind**."

Still, despite these very different views, the Council was able to unanimously congratulate the winner. The dissidents explained their position by saying that they had appointed the judge as referee, and that they must abide by **his** decision.

Comment. This little interchange in Council **reflected a wider argument in society**. There were some who accepted the new so-called modern art, with its "floating spotted triangles and body-less bloodshot eyes". There were others who regarded it as kindergarten art that had no place alongside the grand masters of centuries. Some of these expressed the view that all the great paintings had already been painted years ago, and that no one would ever improve on what already existed.

Be that as it may, this was a controversy that split the art world for decades, and probably still has not died out.

THE HORRORS OF COUNTRY PUBS

For many years it had been accepted by the Oz community that the accommodation in country pubs was atrocious. In any country town, there were as yet no motels, no well-advertised boarding houses, no such things as youth hostels. The only place for the weary traveller was the local pub. Without going into detail, let me just say that whatever it was that you wanted from such an institution, it was missing. Well, almost. You **could** get a bed and blankets. There was one toilet, down the hallway in the bathroom, with the leaking hand-basin, and a much-used bar of Sunlight soap. Not much else. Anyway, who does **actually** need a towel?

These luxuries were not backed up by any display of cleanliness, and civility from the publican was in short supply. Our American friends, coming for the Olympic Games, could not believe their eyes. One of these will have his say in a moment, but I will give you first the view of one person on the current state of the pubs.

Letters, G W Docker. As an active member of a trade, woolbroking, many of whose members are regularly subjected to the horrors of country accommodation in the course of their business, I feel it is not yet too late for a further appeal to both the breweries and that section of the community who are private hotel owners and licensees.

The "pubs" have driven their clientele to form clubs for some form of comfort in those facilities which a club can provide, and poker machines and the like are called to their financial assistance.

Unfortunately, the weary traveller cannot form his clubs, but must seek accommodation in our country hotels.

With some experience, I have no hesitation in stating that conditions in a great majority of cases are substandard. Beds are uncomfortable, evening meal-hours ridiculous, and bath and lavatory conditions in many cases insanitary and a menace to health.

The only improvement of note in many hotels in recent years has been the provision of **inner-spring mattresses**. This Labor-saving device avoids the need for shaking or turning the mattress and is thus welcomed by staff.

If hotels earnestly endeavoured to train their licencees, and improve courtesy, comfort and cleanliness, the present trading hours would enable them to regain their standing to the general benefit of the whole community. The "one-armed bandit" as a tax-raising medium would surely fall away.

The gentleman below gets away from the moaning that we all did about the situation, and comes up with an idea that, in those days, was simply unheard of.

Letters, Roland Hill (American Travel Headquarters), Sydney. Today, probably more than ever before, tourists are interested in their material comfort.

To put the matter in a nutshell, everything depends upon the hotel industry. This being so, it is surely in the best interests of all concerned in obtaining a fair share of the international tourist trade to see that their own hoteliers are accorded every possible assistance and cooperation.

Wise Governments give a ready ear to the suggestions made by hotels, even if it is not always possible to carry them out, either in part or in whole.

In some countries (for example, Turkey, Spain, Mexico, Egypt, West Germany, Thailand, Cuba, Puerto Rico, Uruguay) Governments are providing hoteliers with loans at a low rate of interest, or interest-free, to improve establishments.

Some countries are going a stage further, with Governments finding the necessary finance to build new establishments, offering the amenities which are demanded by first-class travellers.

Air, rail, steamship, and bus lines have been subsidised, or given concessions, either originally or currently, directly or indirectly, over the years.

American travel agents feel that **Australia should subsidise the construction and maintenance of moderate-price hotels, with private shower, bath, and toilet**, if Australia is to participate in a greater reception of American tourists.

Comment. Sixty years later this idea **might** have got a hearing. After all, our economic masters **now** do provide funding for tourism from large budgets, and the nation realises that our continued prosperity is linked to tourist expenditure. **At the time however**, there were few Australians who thought that way, so that this promising idea was never considered.

DECIMAL CURRENCY

There was a growing cry for decimal currency to be introduced to the nation. You might remember that we were still sticking to our Pounds, Shillings and Pence, with a few Guineas and the odd Farthing thrown in. Our British exemplars were doing the same. But in the USA, Dollars and Cents were the order of the day and, of course, this was based on the decimal system.

We were trading more and more with the Yanks. So it is hardly surprising that comparisons of our currencies were starting. At the same time, there were murmurs that we could perhaps change over our system of weights and measures to decimal, and that Kilograms might then replace Ounces and Pounds.

So, as early as 1956, we had two Letters supporting the change of currency. A lady from the Adelaide Hills pointed out that shop assistants were not at all adept at handling the intricacies of multiplying and dividing by all sorts of units. She added that most of our accounting machines in Australia, such as cash registers, had in fact come from overseas decimal countries and **had been**

converted to cater for our odd peccadillos. She thought that it would be an easy task to convert them back.

A second writer echoed the latter point, and looked ahead a little at the future.

Letters, M J Anthony. Every cash register or accounting machine used in Australia is imported from America. Expensive, time-wasting, functional alterations are required before any machine can cope with the intricacies of shillings and pence, and the same alterations seriously decrease the capacity of the machines in many cases. Moreover, adjustments have to be made for each new job, so that the time-wasting process is not confined to the initial adjustment but is a continuing one.

With Australia on the threshold of a huge programme of mechanisation and perhaps automation in the office, I am certain that all clear-thinking businessmen would wholeheartedly support any move by the government to introduce decimal currency.

Comment. Not withstanding the force of these arguments, **I can assure readers** that this nation's habits and indeed affection for Pounds, Shillings and Pence, is so great that there is no way that they will ever be replaced by an abomination imported from America.

KILLING KOOKAS

Letters, A W Cains, RSPCA. Following on recent statements in the Press that New Australians have been killing and eating kookaburras, the RSPCA has received complaints from members.

I wish to point out that kookaburras are protected birds under the law of this State, and I would appeal to members of the general public to submit reports to the RSPCA regarding any cases that come under their notice, and prosecution will follow.

Comment. The hard-done-by New Australians were blamed for many sins they did not commit. Only in the last week, statistics produced by Police Forces round the nation showed that New Australians' crime rates were not at all different from those of Old Australians, except in communities where there were many more males than females. In those cases, the incidence of fights and drunkenness was higher.

But it is true to say, I think, that in the matter of the killing and eating of kookas, our New Australian friends were no more likely to offend than was anyone else.

THE WAR IS OVER

Talks will begin in Canberra today with Japanese Trade reps. **Japan is now our second biggest trading partner.** Last year they took 11 per cent of our exports.

We sell them wool, barley and sugar. They sell us textiles, steel, canned salmon, crockery and toys.

UNIFORM DIVORCE LAWS

Mr P Joske (MP, Lib) said today that **he will introduce a private Members Bill into Federal Parliament** soon. He is seeking to **introduce uniform divorce laws across all the States**. At the moment, **each State has its own laws** relating to divorce, and they vary widely. He expects that 90 per cent of the population will support his Bill.

OCTOBER NEWS ITEMS

Troubles continue for the Labor Party. In NSW, the Democratic Labor Party **(DLP)**, has now broken away from the Labor Party proper, and **is forming a new Party**....

This is music to the ears of **Victorian activist, Mr Santamaria, who was fundamental in forming the DLP** in Victoria a short while ago. The break-away groups are **made up mainly of Catholics,** and consider that **the Communists have too much say in the Labor Party**....

Branches of the DLP are now formed in all States, and it will become **a powerful third Party in Australian federal politics.**

Tennis star **Ken Rosewall will get married on Saturday**. This is **a big event in Brisbane**, and at least 40 police will be on duty to control the expected crowds. He arrived late last night **on a freight plane from Melbourne**, after he missed his scheduled flight. Special provisions were made for him **to travel at freight rates**.

A new anti polio vaccine is now being tested world-wide. The Sabin vaccine is cheaper to produce than the Salk, and a **single dose will last for life**.

A Japanese salvage company bought four hulls of ships **sunk by the Japanese in their first air raid on Darwin on February 19, 1942**....

The company will bring a salvage fleet of 11 ships to Darwin to cut up the three US and one Australian ships from where they lay in deep water. They will be used for scrap in Japan and other Asian countries.

October 21st. **The Oz team for the Olympics was announced.** 79 names were released, including popular choices such as John Landy, Betty Cuthbert, and Marlene Mathews. Shirley Strickland will be there for the third time.

An English woman and her 10 children were found stowed away on a ship going to England. They were found as the *Orsova* travelled between Melbourne and Adelaide....

The woman said she had been in Australia only for five months, but **could not find suitable accommodation for her brood....**

When the ship's crew heard of her plight, **they agreed to forego one day's pay to pay her passage**. The Captain and the Government said this was impossible., **She was sent by train back to Melbourne.**

Australia has just arranged a **50 million dollar loan with the US-based International Bank**. This loan highlights **Australia's difficult financial position....**

We badly need the money to buy **machinery for primary industry and transport services**, but do not have the exports to pay for such equipment. So we borrow. If the **equipment makes more money than the cost of the loan, then it is good business.**

MELBOURNE OUT OF BOUNDS FOR REDS

The Chinese Classical Theatre Company from Communist China had been planning to perform in Melbourne during the Olympic Games. This was a company of world renown that had presented in major capitals of the world, and indeed to Royalty in London.

In mid-October, the Federal Government started to mumble about the dangers that such performances might give rise to. It was pointed out that Melbourne could be host to many people, including possible malcontents who might demonstrate against the Chinese, and disrupt the harmony necessary for the Games.

For example, Communist China was at war with Chiang Kai Shek's Chinese forces in Formosa (now Taiwan). Both nations claimed Chinese sovereignty, and each would be sending its own team. It **might** be that the opera would stir some partisans from these countries to anti-social behaviour.

Then again, China and Russia were not on speaking terms. This **might** upset the apple cart. Then the Americans, who hated the Russians, **might** be stirred into throwing their dim sims round Chinese restaurants. Even Australians **might** join in the mayhem. After all, in Australia there was saturation propaganda stressing how evil and barbaric the Chinese were, and constant debate over whether we should sell them our wheat during their famines. We could, instead, let them starve.

So, the Government put it to the Chinese Theatre Company that they cancel the Melbourne part of their tour. Over a period of a few days, the response from the Theatre

Company started at sulking and saying that we will cancel the entire tour to the rest of Australia. In the end, though, it shrugged its shoulders and said it would probably perform in Brisbane instead.

The whole thing rattled round for a few more days, then it was finally settled by no less a person then our Prime Minister, Bob Menzies. He made a statement **in Parliament** that said the Company would not now visit Melbourne during the Olympics.

"It would be more in accordance with the spirit of the Olympic Games if **controversy was kept in** the healthy rivalry of **the arena**, and that we should avoid anything that would cause differences or acrimonious dispute outside the arena at that time."

Labor's Doctor Evatt reacted angrily. "It brings Australia into world-wide ridicule and contempt, and Australia should be ashamed of itself". The *SMH*, under the heading *Red Faces and Red Opera*, speculated that the Government could have concerns that a Communist Chinese would chase a Formosan Chinese round the arena with a javelin. It went on to say that this ridiculous ban must be rescinded.

Letters, Helen G Palmer. Your sub-leader on the Federal Government's attempt to rule that the Chinese classical drama company may not keep its contract to play in Melbourne during the Olympic Games, and the admirable cartoon on the same page, do something to put this action in perspective.

The Olympic Games has maintained its tradition of being a meeting place of all peoples in friendly competition, and this spirit has always been highly valued and respected by competitors and visitors.

It is a serious affront to the good sense of the Australian and overseas visitors who will be in Melbourne during the visit of this group to suggest that this tradition will be broken. Who, one might ask, is it feared will bring his political prejudices to the Games and exercise them in this extraordinary way?

Surely it is most fortunate that this company, the flower of a long and honoured dramatic tradition acclaimed throughout Asia and Europe, should be able to visit Melbourne at a time when we want the richest cultural opportunities to be available to our visitors.

It is doubtful whether they will appreciate the Federal Government's action in depriving them of the rare experience of seeing this world-famous group of artists.

Letters, H E Ellen. The action of our leaders in banning the appearance of the Chinese Classical Opera Company in Melbourne during the Olympic Games has been criticised as artistic gaucherie.

It is far more than that. It is a first-class diplomatic blunder. It stems from the misguided general attitude of our Government to Communist China.

The Government has been content to follow the US in its ridiculous affectation of regarding the Nationalist rump in Formosa as the Government of China, even to the extent of allowing it to represent China in the Security Council of UN.

We cannot hope to oust the Communist regime of China. The only sensible procedure is to adopt the attitude of "live and let live."

Australia has much to gain, as is evidenced by the report of Mr H G Menzies regarding the good prospects of a profitable export trade with China.

The present ungracious gesture in response to a friendly overture will probably result in sending the members of the opera company back to their homeland to disseminate a sentiment of dislike for Australia and Australians instead of having them return as ambassadors of goodwill.

Comment. The Company performed in Brisbane. There were no riots in Melbourne during the Games. Which goes to show how wise the Government was in banning the Theatre Company.

BRISBANE IS A STRIKING CITY

For six months, the wool industry had been in turmoil. The various tribunals for wage fixing had decided that the rate of pay for shearing a sheep should be cut. This was because the market price for wool had fallen. The tribunals reasoned that when the price went up for the Korean War, the workers had been paid higher rates of pay, so that now when the price had dropped, so too should the wages.

The price paid to shearers affected the rates paid to a string of other workers, such as packers and storemen, transport workers, wharf Laborers and seamen. So **you** will not be surprised that all of these were involved in restoring, and indeed incrementing, the wages of shearers.

The ideas of sensible negotiations and conciliation were not part of the industrial relations system at the moment in Oz, so strikes were called by the dozens of unions that had an interest. The trouble was the problem was so widespread, right across the nation, and there was no focal point. The graziers, too, had an advantage that they could do the shearing themselves, and they could recruit other locals who could do a fair job, so that they could produce the wool ready for the next stage of processing.

The up-coming **Brisbane wool sales** provided the needed focal point. They were a big event on the calendar. It was to these sales that the graziers sent their wool, and it was there that the storemen and packers prepared the wool for the export trade. So, it was at this point that it was decided to mount a major strike. The packers, truckers, wharfies, and seamen all refused to handle **the black wool** that the graziers had organised.

As it turned out, the truckies were of little weight, because there were plenty of non-unionised drivers who were happy to earn a few quid. Likewise, in this case, the seamen were useless, because the ships booked all had foreign crews. But the storemen were ready, and refused work on October 3rd. **700 of them were immediately sacked.** This was a bit of a shock to them.

Premier Gair called a State of Emergency. Over 48 hours, the wharfies declared that they would not handle black wool, and Gair promised to call in troops to do **any** job vacated by a striker.

In the meantime, the wool sales were going on, and after a slow start, were now realising appreciably higher prices. **Gair jumped at this opportunity**. If he persisted with his threat to call in the troops, he would certainly win the strike, but the political back-lash from the unions would haunt him for life.

So he started to equivocate. The wool prices were higher, and that might allow an increase in wages. He was happy for the various tribunals to look at the wages again in this light, and perhaps the brewing head-on collision could be averted. In fact, the strikers were very ready to accept any olive-branch at this stage, and opted to go back to work.

In the long run the workers did get their old rates back, and a bit more as well. This of course flowed through to the other classes of workers.

Comment. This was an action-packed two weeks that held the attention of the nation. It is interesting to note that in this case, strikers **did** gain a small increase in wages. Though not enough to brag about.

What again emerged was that during a strike, attitudes harden, and the **very worst that can come out of a strike is to "lose" it**. When that happens, the union executives **lose face**, and the rank-and-file feel that someone has dudded them, and they are not so ready to strike next time.

THE SUEZ STORY STILL

In October, the Brits stopped their sabre rattling, and decided to talk seriously instead. Of course, in public at the UN they took the stance that an international treaty had been abrogated, and that the wrath of Hell should fall on the Egyptians if they did not change their position.

Half way through the month, it seemed that Britain, France and the US had come up with a formula that might have satisfied the Egyptians. Before the vote-less Egyptians could agree, or not agree, to the proposal, Russia and Yugoslavia voted against it, meaning that Russia had used her UN veto against the so-called six-proposals. Back to the drawing board.

Still, no need to give up. Egypt continued to talk to the two major parties, and by the end of the month, the Brits at least were issuing leaks that said that maybe they were getting somewhere.

Back here in Oz, Letters came thick and fast. Writers were still happy to criticise Menzies, there were many who took the side of all ex-colonies and said that they were justified in claims against their former masters, while a smaller number said that Egypt was bound by a Treaty, and should stick to it regardless of whether or not it was now seen as reasonable.

I will not report on most of those Letters here, but will instead present just one Letter that seems to me to have a lot of sense, even though there is no hope that the real world will ever adopt his position.

Letters, P E Nygh. The present trouble over the Suez Canal shows us clearly what is the most important issue in the world today. Namely, the growing antagonism between Europe and "The Rest."

The fact is that European (in its widest sense) power is receding and that Asia and Africa demand economic as well as political freedom, which, to be completely effective, **requires the nationalisation of all Western assets in these areas**. On the other hand, the highly industrialised west will be at the mercy of the Asian Powers for the vital supply for their industries.

Perhaps the only way out would be to call a conference, not merely on the Suez Canal, but on Western investments in Asia and Africa generally. The West should forestall Asian and African opinion by voluntarily offering to liquidate its positions. We have nothing to lose, as we will lose these positions anyway, but we may gain Asian-African friendship and cooperation.

In return, Asia should recognise the vital interest of European industry in the supply of raw materials.

Comment. At the end of the month, it is probably true to say that the sting seems to have gone out of the Suez. In the normal manner, talks will go on and on, small crises will come and go, and diplomatic victories will be claimed at all times by all parties. But the threat of force has gone away, and so **we can all sleep more soundly in our beds tonight**.

BUT WAIT: HANG ON A MINUTE

What's that you say. **On the last day of the month, Israel has invaded Egypt?** Is that true? Israeli troops are only 20 miles from the southern end of the Canal? The Brits and France have asked Egypt if they can drop paratroops into the Canal zone? Who is writing this scenario? Can we sleep soundly in our beds after all?

Comment. I am afraid we will have to wait till next month to find out.

RUSSIA DEFENDING ITS TERRITORIES

After WWII, Russia took command of about ten nations on the western side of its border. It imposed its Communist economy on them, set up Communist political domination, and placed a large number of bases and troops in each nation. These so-called satellite States were very much subjected to Russian planning and control. All of them objected to this, but were apparently powerless to change the situation.

However, in mid-October, nationalist groups in Poland thought they might succeed in breaking away. They staged a series of military uprisings that continued for a few weeks. In that time, they organised riots in three cities, forced the resignation of a prominent local Red figure and, according to news reports, a Polish woman publicly stomped on a Russian flag. These were small triumphs, and it was clear that the Russians were waiting for a suitable time to stamp out any rebellion.

Still, it inspired similar nationalists in Hungary. Towards the end of the month, more serious conflicts broke out in Budapest, and then other regions, some battles were fought, and **the Hungarians were able to claim that the Russians had been defeated**. In the midst of all this, when the Russians appeared to have the upper hand, the Hungarian team was withdrawn from the upcoming Olympic Games. When the Hungarians were later on top, the team was re-installed.

At the end of the month, it seems too early to proclaim that the Hungarians had ousted the Russians. Russia had a mighty army, and was not at all inclined to enter conflicts without sufficient force. It seemed likely that it would be back, and that when it returned it would do so with enough forces to win an easy victory.

Comment. We will have to wait to see.

IS HE WORTH SAVING?

A lone yachtsman was pulled off a reef in the region of New Guinea, and brought back to shore. He was lucky, because the odds of him being spotted were small, and there was no way he could have survived for long. He was a bit wild in his ways, and wanted to be the first person to sail solo round the world, but gave no indication that he had the capacity to organise or carry out such a venture.

Be that as it may, one woman had thoughts about him. In a rather scatty Letter, she made her position clear.

Letters, Lili Gustav. Let Mr Weil (the lone yachtsman who was wrecked off New Guinea) know that next time he is in a tight spot again, **there will be no Catalinas or Lincoln bombers going to his rescue**, at great expense to the public.

How much is a man's life worth? As much, one might say, as he is honestly trying to make it worth to the public, or to an idea, or to some other person at least outside himself.

Is he an artist whose creative urge is a law to itself? Does he study the rainfall or tribes that he meets on his travels? Does he record the weather, at least for any other purpose except his own benefit?

Even assuming that not he but some newspapers are responsible for the splash that is made of him, does the public have to pay for any egotist's vanity or any stuntsman's holiday, when something goes wrong?

If he really wants to get "away from it all," let him smash his radio and let's have no more of him.

Others were more inclined to offer help.

Letters, R Lock. It would require the services of an actuary to calculate the proportion of the cost of "going to the rescue at great public expense" of Danny Weil to be personally borne by Lilli Gustav, who, by inference, is more concerned with this aspect than the total cost to that abstract entity "the public."

Danny Weil was just out of luck and no real Australian begrudges the cost of giving Danny a break. Were it not for adventurous souls like him with an itch to sail beyond the sunset, there would have been no Empire and particularly that part of it under the Southern Cross.

Letters, M Mclean. In reply to Lili Gustav's letter, may I express the hope that as a nation our outlook has not sunk to the level of counting the cost in the saving a human life?

The assertion that Mr Weil's lone voyage was a stuntsman's holiday or an expression of an egoist's vanity is rather sweeping. Was he breaking any laws? Would he have deliberately piled his yacht on an unseen reef? Is no one entitled to seek his own pleasures, either in solitude or in the mass, without having to determine what is to be gained from it for general benefit?

What of the thousands who frequent our beaches during the summer, and the hundreds that are rescued either from foolhardy or accidental plunges into water beyond their depth? Should they be left to drown because their rescue may endanger another's life and would yield nothing to further the advance of art or science?

I have lived in many parts of this country and in all of it I have found the quickly extended hand and unstinted effort to help those in trouble.

Bushfires immediately attract their hordes of willing fighters. The recent floods have told us their tales of tireless battles when all fought to help each other.

Is a lost hiker or straying child left to perish in the bush? Do the men who hunt for the lost hiker count the cost of a lost day's pay?

Lili Gustav should realise that we don't count the cost of a life or look for payment. We don't even ask if it is a life worth the bother of saving. We just do our best to save it.

ANOTHER COMMENT ON PUBS

Below we have an example of the never-ending complaints about the accommodation in our pubs.

Letters, R J Keegan. A good deal has been written and said recently on the subject of encouraging tourists to visit this country, and in nearly all cases the emphasis has been on providing better hotels. I submit that this is pure speculation; people do not visit a country just to live in its hotels, however luxurious these may be.

I suggest that the magnet, which draws many thousands of visitors each year to Britain and the European continent, is **history and all that goes with it** in the shape of religion, literature, music, early architecture, etc.

In this matter of tourism, the Australasian countries **are up against a lack of history and historical features** (an obvious lack in all young countries) plus geographical remoteness, and while it may be possible to substitute some other attraction for the former, the latter remains a formidable obstacle.

A SAD RESULT

Quadruplets, born to the Eslick parents from the NSW town of Bathurst, **all died last night** in Royal North Shore Hospital in Sydney. They were ten weeks premature, and all died within six hours of birth, despite constant supervision, and the use of four humidicribs that had come from Bathurst.

NOVEMBER NEWS ITEMS

I will leave reports on Suez and Hungary till later in the Chapter. **So that here, I will report my normal news items.**

The Duke of Edinburgh was on his way to the Olympics. He entered Australia **via Darwin**. On his first day here, he spent 40 minutes "talking to 200 brawny, shirtless wharfies" who gave him a resounding cheer as he left. He then spent two hours at the far-away uranium mine at **Rum Jungle**, and drove slowly through the dusty red streets of Bachelor, the local township….

That night, **he went crocodile shooting.** He killed a 6-foot croc with a single shot from a .303 rifle. **The skin will be tanned and sent to Buckingham Palace.** Next day, he was in Alice Springs, where he survived **the 107 degree** heat, and spent hours talking to stockmen and watched the bull-dogging of cattle in their normal working day. It was reported that he **bears the flies better** than any other member of his party….

Two days later he appeared in Canberra, **dressed in the uniform of Marshal of the Royal Australian Air Force**. At a parade and public reception, he met diplomats, Service Chiefs, Cabinet Ministers, and politicians, **many of them dressed in morning dress and top hats**. He, as usual, took all this formality in his stride, but many in the Press commented that **he looked more at home in the sales-ring in Alice**.

All seats have been sold for the Olympics, so now scalpers are active. This apparently surprised the

Sunday Telegraph which ran the front-page story on it on November 18th.

The Olympic torch landed in the fair city of Cairns, and had made its way down to Sydney by November 18th. As it came through **the northern suburbs, 400,000 people** turned out to cheer it on, and **another 200,000 people saw it into Sydney's CBD**. Alderman Pat Hills, the Lord Mayor, accepted it, and passed it on to the next set of bearers who will head towards Melbourne....

The number of spectators is quite extraordinary, just to catch a glimpse of a torch. Of course, it was a once-in-a-lifetime event. It just showed how much **the Olympics had caught the imagination of the Australian public**.

November 22nd. The Games open today. The Duke in a sailor suit, lots of marching girls and boys in pretty uniforms, a torch and a vat of oil, a crowd of 103,000 in a stadium basking in bright sunshine, fanfares of trumpets, and 5,000 pigeons free at last....

There were cheers for all teams, especially the Australians, and big cheers for Russia and other Soviet bloc nations. The USA also got a big cheer. **The Hungarians received a huge ovation** of sympathy. In all, it was a great spectacle, **there were no riots or thrown dim sims**....

Over the next days, records were broken, medal tallies were kept, tears of joy and disappointment were shed, a few angry athletes said they were robbed, Australians were lionised **here**, and **a jolly good time was had by all**.

STILL THE SUEZ

Israel did, in fact, invade Egypt. Her troops charged across the desert, and within a day were within 10 miles of Port Said, on the northern entrance to the Suez Canal. By then, Britain had recovered from the shock, and warned that unless the ensuing war stopped immediately, she would send troops and invade that part of Egypt. The Israelis did stop their advance, but battle continued on other fronts. The two nations were at war.

After a few days, Britain and France sent a large number of paratroops. British aircraft conducted air-raids on Egyptian positions, and their peace-keeping actions included **the sinking of an Egyptian ship in the Canal, thereby blocking it.** A few days later, thousands of British ground troops occupied airfields amid serious battles. As normal during war, both sides at this stage made preposterous claims. The Brits said the Egyptian Air Force had ceased to exist. The Egyptians replied that they had shot down 87 British and French planes.

Over ten days, the three forces engaged in battles, gained and lost territory, and said tough words, but the action was mainly in the desert region. There was no attack on civilians or on Cairo by any party.

In the meantime, world outrage at the Anglo-French invasion grew and grew. The biggest call was that these two nations should withdraw, and leave it to the UN to provide a peace-keeping force to stop the Israel versus Egypt conflict getting out of hand. The Brits argued that their forces were in Egypt solely for purpose of "separating the combatants, and stabilising the region". **Only a few**

deliberately gullible nations accepted this as true. In the UN General Assembly, only four nations (out of 76) gave the Brits the support they asked for. Two of these were Britain and France. Australia and New Zealand abstained.

So, world pressure on the Anglo-French was too big to ignore. They said that they would withdraw, and after a few days, when the UN started to send its peace-keepers, they did so over a few weeks. By the middle of November, hostilities had stopped, and the Egyptians regained control of their badly-damaged airfields.

One problem that remained was that the Canal was blocked, not just by the Egyptian vessel that the Brits had sunk. There were by now ten vessels blocking navigation, and these had been sunk by Nasser's orders as the hostilities went on. If we can't control the Canal, then you can't either. It took six months to get the Canal back to working properly.

The Israelis, however, had not withdrawn. They had stopped fighting, but they were holding on to the territory they had occupied earlier. It seemed that they had been unhappy at the treatment they had been given at the last fracas with Egypt, and hankered to get back territory that was lost then. So now they stayed put. Doubtless, such matters would go on and on into the future.

The affair gradually came to an end. Nasser came out if it quite well. He had given no ground, and had stood up well to the bullying of the most powerful Empire in the world. He became a hero-figure to the emerging nations world-wide. Britain and France lost face and trust in all quarters, while the veto powers in the UN were seen to be farcical.

Comments from all quarters poured into the newspapers. Most of them repeated the same message in different tones of outrage or support. A few more here will give you an idea of what some people thought.

Letters, D Reinsford Moore. As an Englishman, I am for the first time in my life ashamed of my country.

The "Herald" leader of November 1st put the Middle East situation very fairly. Even in a world of power politics and broken promises, the action of Britain and France in making war for purely selfish ends is incomprehensible.

Whatever mitigating circumstances the British Cabinet may be keeping secret, the plain fact remains that forces are being used in defiance of the United Nations for reasons that are extremely dubious.

One can only hope that those who govern Britain will be brought to their senses before it is too late. Even so, the British Commonwealth and the whole Western world will have been divided and severely shaken in their belief in the integrity of Britain's intentions.

This is surely a chance for Australia to come out strongly on the side of moderation and negotiation in international disputes. **The only alternative is the extinction of the human race.**

Letters, J M Thomson. By what possible process of reason has a justifiable protest against blatant aggression been turned into a completely unjustifiable action again the victim of aggression.

What has happened to the traditional British policy of restraint? Why has the nation which has hitherto been the champion of the United Nations suddenly assumed the role of its incipient destroyer, by making moves, not only without reference to it, but completely at variance with the affirmed principles on which it is based? Why has the unity of the Western world been rent asunder by the contemptuous brushing aside of American objections?

It seems to me that Mr Gaitskell's condemnation of the action as one of "incredible folly" is too mild. It is a policy of criminal folly.

Letters, Hilda Salier. You seem to have doubts as to the wisdom of the intervention by the United Kingdom and France in the quarrel between Israel and Egypt.

But there must be many Australians who feel, as I do, glad that Great Britain has taken firm and prompt action in the Middle East and who **rejoice that the government of our own country is supporting her in it.**

Letters, Cuthbert C Finlay. Congrats to the British and French Governments on the firm stand they have taken in the Middle East.

Colonel Nasser is a dictator who has been given ample opportunities and been shown much tolerance to make an equable agreement. Unfortunately, America has not been overhelpful.

We have seen in our time the rise and fall of dictators who wished to take the law into their own hands – Hitler, Mussolini and Stalin – and we know their fates.

I am sure the last thing Britain and France wish is a third world war, but now is the time to call Colonel Nasser's bluff.

Letters, Michael G Cruickshank. Every fair-minded, clear-thinking Australian must feel aghast at our Prime Minister's blind stand behind Britain and France over the Suez Canal.

Israel was the aggressor, Egypt the defender, and Britain and France must surely have been in a solid pact with

Israel. Why else then did Israel so conveniently back down at Britain's ultimatum?

We in Australia are in no position to irk our neighbours, the Americans, upon whom, in the event of war in the South Pacific, we will be entirely dependent. I doubt if we will be able to count upon England for help.

The United Nations was formed by the democratic countries of the world to ensure peace and justice. Britain, a predominant member of this organisation, has now openly violated its entire working functions, and if the remaining members of the United Nations permit Britain and France to succeed in violating the United Nations Charter in this manner, then the entire cause of world peace and justice is lost.

Letters, B A Curteis. While the argument is used that Britain's attack on Egypt is warranted because the Suez Canal is vital to her economic survival, Australians must realise that this very same reasoning could be used as an excuse for an attack on Australia. To the north of our vast and comparatively unoccupied continent, there are millions upon millions of Asians, calling out for additional raw materials, for additional food and clothing supplies and for additional living space, all of which the Asians say are necessary for their survival, and all of which, we Australians know, can be supplied by this country.

1956 INVASION OF HUNGARY

The Russians only stayed away for a few days. There was no way they were going to let some pip-squeak nation like Hungary create a hole in the defensive ring they had built up over the last decade. If one country went, then others would want to follow, and that was not high on Russia's agenda.

So in November they stormed back in, and within two days had 200,000 troops and 6,000 tanks in the Budapest region. Many brave souls fought against them, but they were simply killed. Resistance was useless here, and in the countryside as well. In six days, the revolt was all over, and the purge of the dissidents was under way. Thousand upon thousands of men were arrested and trundled, without any sort of trial, into railway wagons, and sent off to Siberia. Many thousands more crossed the border into Austria, arriving there with nothing but their clothes, and thus began another world refugee problem.

Our own Government said it would take 3,000 refugees, and it declared that the Hungarian athletes at the Games could defect to Australia if they chose. No one initially took up the offer. The athletes continued to compete at the Games, and insisted that every time their flag was called for, that the old pre-Russian flag was used. A nice gesture of defiance from afar, but the reality was that their nation had again been over-run by the dominant Russians, and would stay in subjugation until the Iron Curtain came down.

The UN made loud noises in protest. But in the Security Council, where it mattered, the Russians had a veto and could stifle any sort of combined action against her. Again, the veto powers in the UN showed how easily world politics could negate the howls of outrage from the vast majority of the world's nations.

Again, Letter writers were very vocal

Letters, C Wouters. The "Herald" in its leading article of November 5 has rightly said that Russia has struck at the counter-revolution in Hungary with the speed and venom of a cobra.

Once again the rule of the most ruthless tyrants that history has ever known – of tyrants equal to at least, if not worse than, the Gestapo and the Kempei Tai – is being imposed on a proud and fearless people.

There can be no doubt that the commander of the Russian troops will sooner or later be able to tell his masters in the Kremlin: "There is peace in Budapest." But it will certainly be the peace of a churchyard, as it was the case once with Warsaw in Poland.

It is not exaggerating to say that, by butchering the Hungarian insurgents, Russia has put the clock of civilisation back for centuries.

As a former student of Hungarian civilisation and culture, I can testify that Hungary is one of the countries in Europe that have always been bulwarks of Christianity and civilisation, and I want to pay a tribute of the highest admiration to the defenders of Budapest, the heart of the Hungarian bulwark. I think that it is not to be wondered at that the fiery national credo of the Hungarians, translated into English, is: "I believe in one God; I believe in one fatherland; I believe in the eternal justice of God; I believe in the resurrection of Hungary."

Letters, J Tilden. Of especial interest to Australians is the attitude of Dr Evatt, the alternative Prime Minister. I was among those who regarded him as among the most sincere and successful exponents of justice for all mankind, and I retained my admiration for him, despite the considerable unfavourable publicity he continually receives.

But I am shocked to see that he cannot find it in his heart to condemn, without reservation, the Russians' bloodthirsty suppression of the liberties of the noble Hungarian people.

Letters, Keith Shaw. Dr Evatt has always been consistent in opposition to the resort to force as a means to settle disputes between one nation and another. This is more than can be said of Mr Menzies. Therefore it is both right and logical that no distinction should be drawn between military aggression by the British and French against Egypt, and their defiance of UN principles, and the Russian armed intervention in Hungary.

Letters, Kate O'Connell. It is to our credit that we are sending help to Hungary, but where is our help for Egypt? In spite of the strict censorship shrouding her dead, a little news leaks out occasionally.

We were told by radio on Sunday that there were 1,000 unburied at Port Said. How many have been buried? And what is the number of dead at Port Fuad and other towns? Israel proudly claimed 5,000 Egyptians killed last week; yesterday the number was reduced to 3,000. We can only note that the answer is thousands.

Let us not be led aside by propaganda from either side. It is up to us to think for ourselves. If Britain makes mistakes, we don't need to follow in her steps blindly, but we should help to repair the damage. If we can help the wounded and starving Hungarians, let us also be prepared to help the wounded and starving Egyptians.

THE TORCH: WELCOME

About 200,000 people turned out to watch the Torch come running up to the Town Hall in Sydney. There the Lord Mayor, Pat Hills, waited for the runner. Suddenly he appeared, all sweaty, dressed in singlet and shorts and carrying a flare. He came up to the podium and gave the flare to Hills, then ran off into the crowd.

Hills, blinded almost by the glare of the lights, took only a few seconds to realise it was a hoax, that the flare was indeed just a candle in a jam can, and that the ratbag element at Sydney University has pulled another of their stunts. Hills was not perplexed at all, and readied himself to receive the proper runner.

The City of Sydney Councillors a few days later were not so urbane. They fulminated and threatened to deny Sydney Uni the right to hold their annual Parade next year, but in the long run (three months later) decided to allow the parade.

John and Mary Citizen were mixed in their response to the jape.

Letters, Ronald Winton. Have our City Fathers lost all their sense of humour and proportion? It was practically inevitable that the Olympic torch occasion would stimulate some university student to action.

The bogus presentation was neatly timed and did no harm to anyone – least of all to the Lord Mayor, who is quite capable of dealing with such a situation and has, to his credit, made no frantic public protests.

As a conservative-minded doctor with student days 20 years away, I hold no brief for vandalism, but I fail to see how serious exception can be taken to this piece of minor tomfoolery. In any case, the action of one student should have no bearing on whether or not the student body should be given the opportunity to hold their procession and charity collection next year.

Letters, Sheila Townsend. As a former active member of an English University Student Union, I was shocked and saddened by the flagrant bad taste of the action of a university student on Sunday night when the Olympic torch was about to arrive at the Town Hall. It is tragic that certain irresponsible elements in the student body should bring discredit upon the whole population of Sydney University, as surely this action will have done.

This action deserves severe punishment, for surely such a historic occasion should be kept in the spirit of the Olympic movement and undefiled by adolescent irresponsibility.

Letters, Joseph Cizzio. Congratulations to the young man who hoaxed the Lord Mayor and a crowd of 30,000 waiting the arrival of the Olympic torch on Sunday night.

With his flaming jam tin on a stick, he debunked a pagan cult which has been taken far too seriously.

Certainly he was no more absurd than the Lord Mayor and the Town Clerk in their robes of office solemnly taking part in an anachronistic ritual which the Greeks themselves gave away in the light of Christianity.

To talk about the hoax as being a sacrilege leaves me cold. The Olympic torch is not the Light that will bring peace into the world.

DECEMBER NEWS ITEMS

ATN Channel 7 in Sydney was opened on December 2nd. It was the third Sydney channel to open, though the other two did not withstand the passage of time. The opening was introduced **by a religious invocation**, followed by the National Anthem, then a 20-minute opening ceremony, and a 90-minute variety show….

Melbourne already had one commercial channel and one ABC. These had opened in early November. There was a great number of congratulations all round to persons responsible for the openings, and for opening on time.

The Petrov Affair. Vladamir Petrov and his wife Evdokia were key players in the **Australian spy drama** two years ago. **They have just been granted naturalisation**, and are living under a weak witness protection programme in Melbourne.

The Russians and Hungarians drew to play water polo against each other in the Melbourne Olympics. Their match started alright, with just the usual hidden display of underwater punching, kicking in the kidneys, and verbal abuse….

The Hungarians went to a 4-0 lead, and the Russians got exasperated. Play got rougher, and then **one Russian punched a Hungarian above water**, miles away from the play. Both teams reacted, and pushed and shoved each other, and it looked like a football biff….

The match was officially declared a victory for the Hungarians. The crowd harassed and catcalled the

Russians when they were brave enough to leave the pool. **This was the only major incident to disturb the Games.**

Queensland Health Department has started a campaign against border hoppers. These are NSW residents who live near their common border, but who go to Queensland hospitals for treatment....

This is because **Queensland hospitals' services are free, but fees are charged in NSW.** It is estimated that five per cent of patients cross the border for this purpose.

The unrest in Hungary continues, with the Russians being heavy-handed towards the locals. **Public executions have killed hundreds all over the nation**, and bands of fighters are still hopelessly attacking the Russians....

Melbourne, December 14ᵗʰ. At the end of the Games, many Hungarian athletes are saying **they will not go home.** The Russians have announced that they are **taking family members as hostages**, and that the families will be released only when the athletes return....

December 18ᵗʰ· When the Hungarian team left, **three members remained behind.** A few days later, their light and heat were cut off in their huts in the Olympic village. This did not worry them, because they were **booked for the USA**, where they will do a "**speaking tour coupled with athletic demonstrations**".

TOP AMERICAN MOVIES

The 10 Commandments	Henry Fonda, Dana Andrews
Around the World in 80 Days	David Niven, Shirley MacLaine
Giant	Rock Hudson, Liz Taylor
War and Peace	Deborah Kerr Yul Brynner
Bus Stop	Marilyn Monroe Dan Murray
High Society	Bing Crosby Grace Kelly
The Eddy Duchin Story	Tyrone Power Kim Novak
Love Me Tender	Elvis Presley Debra Paget
The Man Who Knew Too Much	James Stewart Doris Day
Written on the Wind	James Stewart Dorothy Malone

BEST MOVIE: Around the World in 80 Days
BEST ACTOR: Yul Brynner (The King and I)

TOP OF THE POPS

Just Walkin' in the Rain	Johnnie Ray
Que Sera, Sera	Doris Day
The Yellow Rose of Texas	Mitch Miller
Sixteen Tons	Frankie Lane
Memories are Made of This	Dean Martin
Heartbreak Hotel	Elvis Presley
Mack the Knife	Louis Armstrong
The Great Pretender	The Platters
The Wayward Wind	Gogi Grant
Hot Diggity	Perry Como
Rock and Roll Waltz	Kay Starr
The Poor People of Paris	Les Baxter
Moonglow	Morris Stoloff
Be-Bop-A-Lula	GeneVincent
My Prayer	The Platters
Portuguese Washerwoman	Joe Fingers Carr

THE END OF THE OLYMPICS

The Games eventually came to an end. The players (nearly) all went home, and got rousing welcomes everywhere. **Our** boys and girls marched or were driven through the streets of Melbourne, then Sydney, and were cheered by thousands of spectators, and given lunches in Town Halls and similar places. The Gold Medal winners were almost sainted, the Silvers and Bronzes were honoured, and the others also ran.

Australia had a good medal tally, which throughout received as much attention as most athletes. Our girl sprinters did well, and swimmer Murray Rose had a medal count of six (over two Games) the last time I looked.

The organisation and facilities were praised by our overseas guests, as was the friendliness and hospitality of our people. The TV coverage overseas had been patchy, because the dispute between TV producers and the Olympic Committee had never been properly resolved. The TV reception in Australia had been good, and granted that our cameramen were learning on the job, had thrilled the relatively few locals who had managed to buy a new TV set.

Finally, the official films of the Games were played in movie theatres overseas. As was the custom of the day, these films took the form of Movietone news briefs of about two minutes a topic, and were played before the main feature. Sadly, most people agreed that our films were not up to scratch.

Letters, C H Voss, Clamart, Seine, France. It is obvious that the Melbourne Olympic Games authorities are not at all television-minded. They had a unique opportunity to show the Olympic setup, but instead of seeing daily emissions on their screens, the French read, three times a day, a statement to the effect that the Games cannot be shown as the television operations had been prohibited by the Olympic Games authorities. It is easy to realise the impression that the statement in question makes.

As a medium of propaganda, television is unique. Reading about Australia or hearing about Australia on the radio is far different from seeing the real thing on the television screen. No description of shooting the breakers can make a listener realise the incredible beauty of a young god standing on a board on the crest of a huge wave. Such a sight was shown recently in a Paris cinema theatre and the spectators were thrilled. Unfortunately, the film had been made in Honolulu.

Letters, Cecil Holmes, Australian Tradition Films, Sydney. Australia itself stands to lose much goodwill. A golden opportunity has gone astray.

The rights for filming the Games were sold to an obscure New York agent, and the actual filming was handled by, for the most part, people with little or no experience. None of the reputable organisations or leading technicians in this country were involved in making the film. The Department of the Interior film division, the Shell film unit, Pagewood and Avondale film studios, Fox Movietone, and Cinesound played no part at all. Most of the skilled and experienced people associated with these organisations **were not involved**.

The human and technical resources that these organisations together could have provided would have certainly led to the production of a first-class film.

Ironically, technicians in this country have acquired over the years a special skill in covering all kinds of sport, and would have been very much at home in making a document on the Games. As well, the poor and inadequate newsreel coverage that found its way into a few theatres also reflects little credit on those responsible. Badly exposed negative, dull angles, and a very ordinary sound track together made this great event sometimes seem like a country sports meeting.

What is so scandalous is the fact that many millions of people all over the world could have seen a fine record of the Games and an immense amount of goodwill could have accrued to Australia. Now it appears that nothing like this will happen; on the contrary, a rather poor impression instead will be conveyed to those who do see the official film.

Still, there was at least one fan who was satisfied.

Letters, (Mrs) W Horsley. Before the Olympic picture fades entirely from Australian minds, I have been hoping to see adequate commendation given to the ABC for the amazing coverage it gave.

I was truly delighted that I was able to follow what was happening at each arena of the Games. Thanks to the excellent descriptive powers of the commentators and the excitement in their voices, we felt we were with them on the sidelines.

I went to Melbourne for one day in the second week, and, thanks to my extensive course of Olympic broadcasts, the scene and buildings and general layout seemed quite familiar to me.

Comment. I should mention again that the **idea of copyright** on public events, like the Olympics and sporting fixtures, became a real issue that has bugged a few entrepreneurs ever since.

OVERSEAS MATTERS

Of course, the two overseas areas of concern are still Egypt and Hungary. **In Egypt**, the Brits and France are frothing at the mouth, but they are withdrawing their troops. Nasser has weathered the storm, and will get more revenue than before from the Canal, and importantly, he will be in control of an enterprise on his own land. The whole **Third World** has applauded his actions, and has learned that it can stand up to its colonial masters. The **First World** learned its lesson too, and will hesitate in future to strong-arm its former possessions.

Russia played the Suez crisis adroitly. Here and there it talked tough against the Anglo-French alliance, but it mainly kept out of it. It had its eyes on winning the Third World over to its side in the Cold War. It went out of its way to support Egypt financially during the crisis, and for years after. It lost no friends during the fray, and many unattached smaller nations noted that Russia might be of help if they ended up in a fracas with a Great Power.

America also stayed out of the way. In November it had its Presidential elections, and no candidate was going to lose votes by acting forcefully on a matter far from the home shores. Beyond that, a disinterested nation was split on who were the goodies and who were the baddies, so that there was little American actual involvement. Again, like the Russians, it was concerned with recruiting the Third World to its cause.

In Hungary, the death toll mounted during the month, as patriots (or insurgents) mounted attacks on the invaders. These achieved nothing, and only increased the reprisals.

The end result was that the Russians maintained strict control for decades, and sadly this control was more severe than prior to the uprising.

THE UN UNDER THE MICROSCOPE

The United Nations' reputation suffered badly. In both Egypt and Hungary, the Brits and then the Russians were widely seen as being enormous bullies picking on small helpless innocents. In Hungary in particular, world anger grew as more reports emerged from the embattled nation. The question being asked by tens of millions worldwide was why doesn't the UN step in and stop it.

The answer, which most protestors **would** not hear, was that to do so might have started a third World War, and this time with atomic weapons. No one knew just how far the Reds would go to keep their protective ring of countries around their western borders, but everyone knew that they would not give them up lightly. Would they go to a limited war to retain the ring? Could the limited war turn into an atomic war? No one knew the answer, but none of the responsible governments of the world wanted to take the risk.

So the Russians were able to march on. The other nations tut-tutted, a few imposed economic sanctions for a while, but the Russians did not blink. **The UN, meanwhile, was full of bluster, but powerless to act.** Many people asked what use it was if **might was clearly right**. Surely, its purpose was to **deny that doctrine**, and that the very rationale for its existence was to ensure that **the rule of right, and not the rule of wrong, prevailed in all situations, big and small.**

A few Letters show some of the arguments.

Letters, S M Pruden. The war ended not last year but over 11 years ago, since when a vast new skyscraper has been built in the United States to house the UN, and millions must have been spent on the excessively high salaries of UN personnel. In the same period, Russia has gained the political domination of China, still threatens in Korea, has annexed the Balkans and Eastern Germany, practically obliterated Hungary and moved into the Middle East. When, to put it bluntly, are we going to get our money's worth out of the UN?

How far can one go in meeting the terrors and atrocities suffered by a persecuted nation with the neat platitudes of the UN? **Where is its police force**, and where its real power to protect all the smaller nations?

Letters, George Baker. The West, Australia with it, cannot indefinitely stand by, applauding the courage of Hungarians and other East Europeans, while the Russians butcher them. A particularly sickening feature of the Wests' conduct has been its use of the UN, which was established to curb aggression, as an excuse and an instrument of appeasement.

To anyone who looks back even on Twentieth-century history, this appeasement of the Reds is evident madness. It may postpone internal and external conflicts with them, but only at the cost of making them in the end more certain, and because so much is being surrendered in the meanwhile, in the end more difficult to fight.

I do not advocate the immediate declaration of war upon the Communist Powers, but suggest they be told that if they storm or subvert a free State, we shall fight them until one side is beaten, and that they must permit free elections in their restive satellite states, and that they must withdraw their subversive influence from such places as Indonesia and the Middle East.

What is patently insane is to make war more probable by continuing to appease the Communist Power; and we ought to have the prudence and courage to stop it at once.

To do so will be, admittedly, to risk war; not to do so will be to make certain either war or bloodless, gutless surrender. We have nothing to lose by stopping appeasement and we may gain peace.

SUMMING UP 1956

Anyone with a good long-term memory remembers 1956 for four events. The Olympics, the introduction of TV into Oz, the Suez crisis, and the Hungarian revolution. As it turns out, all four of them occurred in the last two months of the year, thereby turning a quite ordinary year into one that became quite exceptional.

In the middle of all the headlines that they occasioned, however, life went on in the nation. It might be hard to realise after the coverage of the last few months, but the strikes of the earlier months continued on very healthily throughout. So too did the prosperity that Australia managed to maintain, year after year. Jobs were plentiful, kids were always ready to make their debut on life's stage, new cars or even second cars could be brought on HP, and my old favourite, Hills Hoists, kept popping up in new suburbs. The community was largely happy, the more unfortunate had a safety net that was adequate, and far better than in most countries of the world. The chronically sick and the infirm and the disabled did have some form of assistance that kept body and soul together. Again, this was better than in most parts of the world.

As to the future, I happen to know that in the next year, epoch making events were restricted to the reduction in the number of lads conscripted to National Service, "The Pub with no Beer" won Australia's first gold record, and there was an outbreak of the dreaded Asian flu. The following year, equal pay for women (for equal work) was legislated for, the first Australian canned beer was sold, and Albert Namatjira was sentenced to six months gaol for supplying liquor to another Aborigine. All of these were interesting events, but hardly on the late 1956 scale.

If you were born in 1956, you can claim to have had an adventurous start to life. You can also look forward to at least ten years of low controversy (until the Vietnam War), and indeed to many years more **after that**. So, given the surrounding prosperity, and the fair chance of a war-free Australia, you are off to a good start, and I hope that over the years, things just keep getting better and better.

Born in 1969?
What else happened?
Australian Social History

HARD COVER

Ron Williams

In 1969, Hollywood produced a fake movie that appeared to show a few Americans walking on the moon. Laborites should not worry because Paul Keating just got a seat in Canberra. Thousands of people walked the streets in demos against the Vietnam War, and HMAS Melbourne cut a US Destroyer in two. The Poseidon nickel boom made the fortunes of many, and the 12-sided cupro-nickel 50cent coin filled the pockets of our new but ubiquitous jeans. Oz Magazine died an untimely death.

****

ORDER FROM ALL GOOD BOOK STORES

AND NEWSAGENTS

OTHER BOOKS IN THIS SERIES

In 1958, the Christian brothers bought a pub and raffled it; some clergy thought that Jesus would not be pleased. Circuses were losing animals at a great rate. Officials were in hot water because the Queen Mother wasn't given a sun shade; it didn't worry the lined-up school children, they just fainted as normal. School milk was hot news, bread home deliveries were under fire. The RSPCA was killing dogs in a gas chamber.

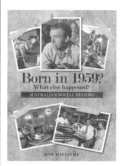

In 1959, Billy Graham called us to God. Perverts are becoming gay. The Kingsgrove Slasher was getting blanket press coverage. Tea, not coffee, was still the housewife's friend. Clergy were betting against the opening of TABs. Errol, a Tasmanian devil, died. So too did Jack Davey. There are three ways to kill a snake. Aromarama is coming to your cinema.

****

Chrissi and birthday books for Mum and Dad and Aunt and Uncle and cousins and family and friends and work and everyone else.

Don't forget a good read and chuckle for yourself.